Dr. Bruce H. Wilkinson

TEACHING

APPLIED PRINCIPLES OF LEARNING SERIES

WITH STYLE ®

"Great teachers,
1 teaching Biblically-based truth
2 with creative methods,
3 see lifechange occur
around the world!"

Bruce H. Wilkinson

Take a fresh look with me at our Lord's final command to His disciples (which includes us, by the way!):

"Go therefore and make disciples of all the nations, baptizing them in the name of the Father and of the Son and of the Holy Spirit, teaching them to observe all things that I have commanded you; and lo, I am with you always, even to the end of the age."
(Matthew 28:19-20)

"Go" is our life's activity as Christians. "Make disciples" is the ultimate result of our going. "Baptizing" is a one-time event bringing new believers into church fellowship.

Then there is "teaching." Here we come to the day-in, day-out, heart-and-soul of Christ's Great Commission. Teaching is it! How effectively we fill the whole world with new disciples, and how mature those disciples ultimately become, is in large part a function of how we teach!

I hope you catch a glimpse in this brief space, and in the course you are about to enjoy, of what a serious task we have, and how absolutely crucial—perhaps *eternally* crucial— teaching is in God's grand scheme of things.

All Christians are called to teach. I believe this with all my heart! Are you a parent? You teach your children. An employer? You teach your workers. A school teacher? Your students. A pastor? Your flock. We are all called to teach someone, somewhere, because we are called to make disciples, which is accomplished through teaching.

I am so committed to this proposition that I have dedicated my life to providing tools and training for those who teach the truth of the Word

DR. BRUCE H. WILKINSON
is the founder and
president of Walk Thru
the Bible Ministries.

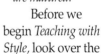

of God to others.

The fact that you hold this Course Workbook in your hands shows you are motivated to learn to teach better. Apply yourself to the principles you learn in this course and you will teach for lifechange, and wonderfully help fulfill our Lord's final command to His church—*to teach so that all over the world new disciples are made and older disciples are matured!*

Before we begin *Teaching with Style,* look over the next few pages. They will give you a glimpse of Walk Thru the Bible's commitment to helping the Body of Christ teach for lifechange.

Whoever you are called to teach, you will teach them more effectively after this course. God bless you as you prepare to serve the Lord!

Great teachers communicate...
1 Biblically-based truth

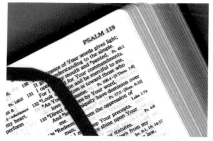

Walk Thru the Bible Ministries has a central word in its name: *Bible*. The Scriptures form the source of what we believe as an organization, and what we achieve as a ministry. The Bible is indeed the foundation of Walk Thru the Bible and all the tools it produces.

The motivation for the ministry's founding in 1976 was the dream of a young seminary student named Bruce Wilkinson to teach people an overview of the entire Bible in such an effective way that they would never forget it.

Thus, the *Walk Thru the Old Testament* and *Walk Thru the New Testament/400 Silent Years* seminars were born and have been hosted by thousands of churches worldwide.

A new appreciation for Scripture from a Walk Thru seminar can be continued with one or more of Walk Thru's seven devotional magazines—*The Daily Walk, Closer Walk, Quiet Walk, LifeWalk, Family Walk, Youthwalk*, and *Tapestry*. Personal Bible reading can be enhanced by several specialty study Bible editions, and children can learn the names and themes of each Bible book through the *Keyword Learning System*. There's a Bible tool for everyone!

The course you are about to study, *Teaching with Style*, is part of Walk Thru's International Video Bible Curriculum. Whether seminars, magazines, or video, the Bible is the basis!

Walk Thru the Bible is a non-denominational ministry standing squarely in the mainstream of historic, orthodox Christian belief. Walk Thru's products and tools have been used by churches in every major Protestant and Catholic denomination and tradition. The seminar faculty consists of graduates of every major American seminary, and many other evangelical ministries adapt Walk Thru's magazines and curriculums for use with their own members and constituents.

Mission Statement of Walk Thru the Bible:
Walk Thru the Bible Ministries exists to contribute to the spiritual growth of Christians worldwide through Bible teaching, tools, and training.

Great teachers use...
2 Creative methods

Fun

Walk Thru seminars are total learning experiences. Sight, sound, and action become memory pegs for acquiring and storing critical content.

Effective

From the beginning, Walk Thru the Bible has believed that it is the teacher's responsibility to cause students to learn. Therefore, when Walk Thru teaches, regardless of the format, an attempt is made to teach creatively—with style! Walk Thru's live seminars are designed to keep participants' attention and cause learning and retention of content to take place. More than one and a half million people, in more than one hundred countries, have attended and benefitted from Walk Thru's live seminars.

The two original seminars, *Walk Thru the Old Testament* and *Walk Thru the New Testament/400 Silent Years*, are unique. Using a combination of audience participation, hand signs, mnemonic devices, and creative review techniques, attendees learn and remember the entire scope of Biblical content—all in a matter of hours!

Even children can benefit from these creative learning adventures. The *Kids in the Book* seminar for ages 6-12 teaches children, at their own level, the major people, places, and themes of Scripture.

Two more live seminars, especially for teachers, are *Teaching with Style* and *The 7 Laws of the Learner*. Both of these seminars prove that learning can be fun after all—for teachers and for students!

Regardless of which live seminar you attend, you'll discover that learning can indeed be an exciting adventure!

Walk Thru produces video curriculum using the latest digital production technology.

Powerful

Great teachers see . . .
▣ Lifechange occur around the world!

All around the world, Walk Thru instructors teach thousands of seminars to hundreds of thousands of people.

Christ's command to go into all the world and teach is taken literally by Walk Thru the Bible Ministries. It can be truthfully said that the sun never sets on Walk Thru's ministry around the world.

At the end of 1993, Walk Thru's live seminars were being taught by trained and certified instructors in 25 languages and 35 countries. The popular *Walk Thru the Old Testament* seminar will be taught over 2,500 times on six continents in 1994, with numbers increasing annually. To service an ever-expanding worldwide ministry, Walk Thru has directors and field offices in six major international cities.

The launching of the International Video Bible Curriculum in 1993 provides the foundation for decades of future Biblical teaching around the world. This far-reaching project is designed to provide access to Biblical teaching by the world's largest language groups. Using television, video cassettes, and other visual and interactive media, Walk Thru will distribute creative and attractive Biblical teaching on a catalog of subjects meeting needs the world over.

One of the first successful deployments of the IVBC has been to Russia with The CoMission, a multi-agency people-lift of teachers and Biblical teaching materials to the former Soviet Union.

Global

Trans cultural

"Go therefore and make disciples of all the nations . . . teaching them to observe all things that I have commanded you; and lo, I am with you always, even to the end of the age."
(Matthew 28:19-20)

Go!

Just When You Wished Someone Would Create a Biblically-Based Curriculum for Teacher-Training, Walk Thru Did!

Teaching With Style is only one course you need in your quest to become a master communicator. An entire curriculum—the *Applied Principles of Learning* series—is being developed to provide unique training tools for teachers and all who communicate.

Whether you are a pastor, Sunday school teacher, private or public school teacher, Bible Study leader, coach, trainer, employer, or parent, you will benefit from the Biblically-based principles presented by two of America's outstanding communicators, Dr. Bruce H. Wilkinson and Dr. Howard G. Hendricks. *Teaching with Style* and *The 7 Laws of the Learner* can be taught in a live class setting, while all three seminars can be purchased in video format for use in Sunday school classes, adult studies, or workshops.

The 7 Laws of the Learner presents, in fourteen sessions, the seven principles which will cause your students to learn. **The 7 Laws of the Teacher** demonstrates the seven characteristics by which all great teachers are measured. The newest in the *APL* curriculum series, **Teaching With Style,** shows how to overcome the greatest obstacle to learning today—boredom!

The *Applied Principles of Learning* are just waiting to be applied—by you!

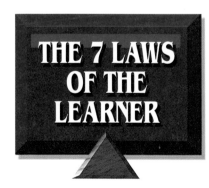

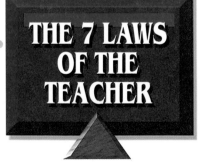

APL — APPLIED PRINCIPLES OF LEARNING

THE 7 LAWS OF THE LEARNER

TEACHING WITH STYLE

THE 7 LAWS OF THE TEACHER

A Profile of STYLE

▶ 1. WHO is TEACHING WITH STYLE for?

Teaching with Style is not just for teachers! Unless, of course, you would agree that everyone is a teacher at some time.

Perhaps you are a full-time teacher, instructor, or even a professor. *Teaching with Style* is definitely for you. But even if you don't teach professionally, this seminar will be of tremendous value.

Parents, pastors, camp counselors, volunteer teachers, Sunday school teachers, Bible study leaders—plus other group and organizational leaders—all have seen how much more effective their communication becomes when they do it with *STYLE!*

▶ 2. WHAT is TEACHING WITH STYLE?

A six-part course designed to eliminate the #1 worldwide hindrance to learning: BOREDOM!

This course is presented in one of two formats: video or live teaching sessions. Regardless of which you attend, you will never communicate or teach the same way again.

The Bible is the basis for *Teaching with Style* for two reasons:

1. Jesus Christ is universally acclaimed as history's most effective teacher.
2. The Bible is filled with examples of God's effective and creative communication with mankind.

Therefore, where better could we look for insight into communicating with STYLE than in the Scriptures—the record of God's creative revelation of Himself to mankind!

▶ 3. WHERE did TEACHING WITH STYLE originate?

Have you ever heard anyone say, "Jesus sure is a boring person!?" Or how about this: "Wow! The Lord was really present in the church service tonight! But it was awfully boring."

You've probably never heard either! If God is never boring, why are His earthly ambassadors (teachers) not as equally dynamic?

That question in the heart of Dr. Bruce Wilkinson prompted a study lasting several years. The quest was to find what makes God such a powerful (NON-BORING!) communicator, and then teach people His methods.

The result? *Teaching with Style*!

▶ 4. WHEN can TEACHING WITH STYLE be used?

The live version of *Teaching with Style* is best for larger church groups (for example, a church-wide presentation) or denominational, organizational, or city-wide seminars.

The video seminar format will be the most widely used because of its simplicity and efficiency. Any small group, Sunday school class, Christian school faculty, individual teacher, or others interested in improving their communication skills can now do so with ease and convenience.

▶ 5. WHY should you attend each session of TEACHING WITH STYLE?

Here's what will happen when you faithfully attend all six of the *Teaching with Style* sessions, live or video format:

- You will be awakened to the most vital need in teaching today.
- You will be taught the universal principles of style.
- You will learn the Biblical characteristics of style.
- You will discover how to possess the internal beliefs of style.
- You will learn to make your body your greatest teaching asset.
- You will see that anyone, regardless of personality type, can teach with style.
- You will learn how to use the same methods Christ did in His teaching.

▶ 6. HOW does the TEACHING WITH STYLE seminar work?

Whether you attend a live or a video seminar, in each of the six sessions your Course Workbook will direct you through the following:
- Take notes on the session's content.
- "Discussion" questions to use with a group or on your own.
- Seven daily devotions taking you into the Scriptures for "style-study."
- A challenging set of projects: choose the right level for you.
- An opportunity to make a commitment to apply what you've learned in the session—to move ahead and Teach with Style!

UNIVERSAL
PRINCIPLES

Great people live by time-honored principles. The same is true of great teachers. Are your principles the Universal Principles of Style? There's one way to find out—turn the page!

INSTRUCTION

Tony Gibbs

"Don't just throw the seed–grind it, bake it, slice it, and put a little honey on it."

Charles H. Spurgeon

PRINCIPLE 1

Style is the process by which the teacher delivers the subject to the _student_.

How the what gets to the who.

"what"   "who"
Subject   student   "how"
                ↑ +   style +
         ← - Teacher - →

The Parsley Effect

PRINCIPLE 2

Style is the primary cause of student _problem_ or _excitement_.

← *Not a content problem.*

PRINCIPLE 3

Style is the responsibility of the teacher and is within the teacher's complete _control._

PRINCIPLE 4

Style is influenced by personality but is controlled by the role the teacher _selects_ .

PRINCIPLE 5

Style should be consciously planned according to the boundaries of the _subject_ _size_ , _setting_ , and _seniority_ .

Noting the flagging interest of his student, Prof. Runlong throws himself into his delivery—

but still misses the mark!

PRINCIPLE 6

Style is fluid and must be adjusted according to the response of your _audience_ .

I do not object to people watching their watches while I'm teaching. I do object when they start shaking them.

PRINCIPLE 7

Style is a learned skill and can be significantly improved through _understanding_ and _practice_ .

It can be k

1 Tim 4:13-15

Ignorance, Intimidation, Indifference, Inhibition

CONCLUSION

A Mastering the Minimum

What was the main point of this session? Try to capture in two to three sentences the "Big Idea." (Hint: what was the subject? What was said about the subject?)

_____

_____

_____

B Perspectives on the Principles

Evaluate your teaching style below in light of the seven Universal Principles. (Record your score in the space.)

Never	Seldom	Sometimes	Usually	Always
1	2	3	4	5

" Hello! My name is Max, and I teach with STYLE! I'm here to encourage YOU to teach with style, too. If you apply what you learn in this course, your teaching will never be the same! **"**

1. I devote planning time in my lesson preparations to deciding which style will best deliver my content.   (____)

2. When my students seem bored, the first thing I check is the style I am using.   (____)

3. I practice the principle of deliberately choosing how I will act in class (vs. "just being myself").   (____)

4. I consistently differ in my role as teacher from other roles in life I must fulfill.   (____)

5. In my lesson/content preparation, I evaluate subject, size, setting, and seniority before teaching.   (____)

6. I change styles easily while teaching based on the students' response to my content.   (____)

7. In the course of a year, I participate regularly in activities designed to increase my teaching skills.   (____)

Add up your total points and enter your score in the margin.

My score: [____]

30 – 35 Expert: making principles a priority!

25 – 29 Advanced: your students appreciate you!

20 – 24 Intermediate: could go either way!

15 – 19 Beginner: unclear on the concept!

10 – 14 Boring: what was the question?

C A Person of Principles

Have you ever known a teacher or speaker who was low-key and reserved out of class but in class was a dynamo? Contrast this person's "everyday" personality with their teaching style:

Normally he or she is . . .

_____

But in class he or she is . . .

_____

Which principle from this session was the teacher implementing? (Rewrite the principle here in your own words.)

_____

D Are Your Principles Showing?

If your students thoroughly understood the seven Universal Principles, they would choose number _____ as being the principle most evident in your life.

They would choose number _____ as the one needing the most improvement.

Try to recall a student conversation or incident which led you to answer as you did above:

_____

E Planning to Practice the Principles

In the area you cited for improvement in D above, write down two steps you can take this week to make progress:

1. _____

2. _____

"Okay—have you got a grip on the Universal Principles? Great! Now, get a grip on your Bible as you prepare for some daily insights from the Word."

Style Delivers the Subject to the Students

Teacher "OK, everybody," Carla Mattland teases in her best I'm-the-teacher-and-I-mean-it voice. "Let's have a seat, please. It's time for our meeting to begin."

Carla, age 30, is excited about this group and its potential. This "class" isn't composed of the elementary pupils she teaches by day at a Christian school. Instead, this is a class of teachers—six men and women in addition to herself, all experienced teachers in various settings:

- *Denise Farris, age 60, currently teaches a seniors adult Sunday school class.*
- *Angelo Perez, 32, is a public high school science teacher.*
- *Pastor Richard Douglas, 45, teaches and preaches in various settings.*
- *Gayle Henson, 38, is a Christian education director teaching young teens.*
- *Steven Kirby, 50, a businessman, leads a lunch-hour Bible study in his office.*
- *Liz Darby, 43, teaches a weekly Bible study for middle-adult singles.*

"While we're a diverse group," Carla begins, "there's actually a way that we're all very much alike."

"Right—overworked and underpaid!" Steven jokes. Everyone in the group laughs and nods.

"Not exactly what I had in mind," Carla says laughing. "We're alike in that we are the living links between our students and the content of our class lessons. Our students all wear 'style-colored glasses,' so to speak, through which they view the lesson. Our teaching style can cause them to see the content as exciting, relevant, and lifechanging—or just the opposite!"

Truth / Hebrews 1:1–2 God knows the importance of style. Throughout recorded history, He has used a wide variety of styles in His communications with people:

> **"God, who at various times and in different ways spoke in time past to the fathers by the prophets, has in these last days spoken to us by His Son."**

In His own teaching ministry, Jesus revealed some of the limitless ways that all teachers can deliver content to their students. He is a model for style.

Transformation Think of it! The world's greatest teacher—Jesus Christ Himself—has offered to live in the heart of anyone who asks (Revelation 3:20)! If our individual gifts and abilities become empowered by His style, watch out! Our classrooms, homes, businesses, and pulpits may never be the same!

Why not pause right now and invite Jesus Christ to walk with you and bring forth His fruit through you as you learn to Teach with Style!

You can become a strong link in God's chain of great teachers.

> ▶ **Develop a "Style" mindset daily as you discover from Scripture how the Universal Principles can make a difference—in _your_ teaching!**

2

D A Y

Boring or Exciting, the Choice is Yours

Teacher "OK, since we're supposed to help each other in this group," Angelo volunteers, "I could sure use help in my science class. I'm boring my students to death with the periodic table of chemical elements—and other not-so-exciting scientific facts. Does anyone have any suggestions for teaching science with style?"

"Well, Angelo," Carla replies, "I had some pretty exciting teachers when I was growing up. They found ways to make their subjects fun. I remember the words to a song that my geography teacher taught us to the tune of 'Yankee Doodle.' It helped us learn the names of the continents in no time flat! I can still remember it today." Carla sings the song perfectly, and the group spontaneously applauds.

"That's great, Carla. But what's the point?" Angelo asks.

Richard interjects, "No offense, Angelo, but it's not chemistry that is boring your students. Content is not 'boring' or 'exciting.' It's just, well, it's just content. Students think they're reacting to content, but actually they're reacting to our presentation of content."

Truth / Matthew 1:17 "Average" content in the hands of a teacher with style is more exciting than a "hot" topic taught in a lifeless way. Take the genealogies in the Bible, for example—when did you last hear a lesson on them? But in the first century, learning genealogies was vital. And Matthew presented them with style:

> **"So all the generations from Abraham to David are fourteen generations, from David until the captivity in Babylon are fourteen generations, and from the captivity in Babylon until the Christ are fourteen generations."**

Many scholars believe Matthew put the genealogical names in groups of 14 to make it easier for early Christians to remember the material. In other words, he presented a difficult and possibly boring subject in a style his readers would find helpful and memorable.

Transformation All truth, whether revealed in God's Word or our world, is important and therefore potentially exciting to students. All content is stimulating when its importance is creatively revealed.

What content are you planning to communicate in the weeks ahead? Regardless of what that content is, take the approach from now on that *content is not boring!* If you can agree with that principle, you are ready to pray and plan toward a creative and exciting approach to teaching your class. Who'd have thought "Yankee Doodle" could help teach geography?

> As long as you've got the choice, choose to do something great!

> **There is no such thing as an uninteresting subject; there are only uninterested people.**
>
> Dr. Duane Litfin

Who's Responsible for My Style?

Teacher Denise has been quiet during the first two meetings—that's her temperament. She's wondering whether changing her style is really her responsibility—or really within her ability.

"I don't know about all this," Denise says hesitantly. "I'm basically a shy person. That's the way God made me. Should I be concerned about having a lot of creative energy and style when it's obviously not 'me'?"

"Now Denise, I've seen you exhibit a lot—I mean a *lot*!—of creative energy, and do it with style!" Gayle says. "I remember seeing you jump up and give the umpire your creative and energetic opinion at your grandson's ball game. Remember that? You decided something needed to be said—and you said it. Now was that the Denise that God made, too?"

Denise chuckles. "I guess you've got a point, Gayle. I've just never thought about bringing that kind of energy into the classroom."

Truth / John 8:6b The Pharisees hoped to incriminate Jesus by His own words when they questioned Him about a woman caught in adultery. Instead, His style won the day. Knowing He had but a moment to communicate His truth, Jesus masterfully took control of the situation.

"Jesus stooped down and wrote on the ground with His finger, as though He did not hear."

Knowing His answer would either end or escalate the confrontation, Jesus took responsibility for getting and keeping everyone's attention. By His unusual action of writing in the sand, He created the moment, and captured the audience. His style left the woman's accusers speechless!

Momentarily put on the defensive by the "students," Jesus the teacher turned an accusation into a teachable moment for His purposes. His dramatic stoop and silent pause became the bow for launching His arrow of truth—right into the hearts of the Pharisees.

Transformation Have you ever concluded from a personality test or some other source that you weren't created for style? Don't believe it. God has given you the two requirements for teaching with style: a sense of responsibility and the ability to choose.

Think back over the past month. Try to recall the wide variety of emotional styles which you expressed in different settings and circumstances—some planned, some spontaneous. Now think about your teaching—was there the same variety and range of expression?

If not, reclaim your responsibility and go on the offensive! Ask God to help you recognize the teachable moments and seize them—with style!

> The pros do the basics well every day.
>
> Vince Lombardi

Exciting teaching doesn't just happen—it's planned that way.

Filling the Role of Teacher

Teacher Like Denise, Liz Darby wonders whether teaching with style applies to her—but for a slightly different reason.

"I'm not an especially demonstrative person—more of a 'thinker' than a 'feeler,'" she says to the group. "And I have doubts about the integrity of teaching in what I regard to be an unnatural way. To be honest, I don't think I have to be somebody I'm not naturally in order to be a good teacher."

"Let me go out on a limb with a suggestion," Richard interjects. "We keep talking about personality types—quiet or loud, outgoing or reserved, whatever. I don't think that's the point at all. Regardless of our personalities, we all fill many different roles every day. We're employees, spouses, parents, friends, committee members—the list is endless! In those settings, none of us changes our personality. Instead, we change our *actions* to match the *role* we are filling. Shouldn't we just view teaching as another of those roles that we fill, with its own requirements for success?"

Truth / 1 Corinthians 9:19, 22 In order to preach the Gospel with maximum effectiveness, Paul had to assume different roles. **"For though I am free from all men, I have made myself a servant to all, that I might win the more; . . . . I have become all things to all men, that I might by all means save some."**

Paul wanted to deliver the most important message in history—the message of salvation through Christ. He wanted people to be saved! In order to do this successfully, he tailored his presentations to the different groups of people he preached to—without giving up his personality or his integrity. He was not being double-minded, he was being multi-faceted. He allowed the need of his audience to determine his style. His chief task was to be flexible and determine the role needed at a given time.

Transformation What words would you use to describe the five key roles in your life that you fill on a daily or weekly basis? Go ahead—use the margin of this page and jot them down. Surprised at how flexible you really are? Did you include "teacher" in your list?

What we're really talking about is job descriptions, aren't we? Do those with whom you live and work *need* for you to fill your roles energetically and with style? Of course—they would feel slighted if you didn't. And what about your students? You're exactly right. They *need* for you to fill your role as teacher—which encourages them to fill their role as learner!

Whisper a prayer to God right now: *Lord, help me fill my role as teacher!*

Great teachers learn to "role" with their hunches.

> To play a role is to affirm the worth of an end.
>
> Oliver Wendell Holmes

Teaching Within the Boundaries

Teacher "I made a serious mistake as a younger teacher," Steven says. "Maybe I can help you avoid making the same blunder.

"My Bible study at work was attended by many executives from throughout the community—men and women. There was a very low level of intimacy and trust among the people attending—most of them hardly knew each other.

"One day I taught a study on sexual purity similar to one my pastor had done with some of the leaders in our church. I used a very graphic style in sharing my material, thinking I could hold people's attention. What I did was keep their attention through embarrassment! The level of openness in that group was not sufficient for the graphic and personal style I used.

"It was the right topic and right group—but definitely the wrong style!"

Truth / Acts 21:40–22:1 Paul varied his teaching style according to the boundaries of subject, size, setting, and seniority even more than we might imagine. For instance, when threatened by Jewish crowds persecuting him for his faith, Paul adapted the style of his message to conform to the culture of his audience.

> **"Paul stood on the stairs and motioned with his hand to the people. And when there was a great silence, he spoke to them in the Hebrew language, saying, 'Men, brethren, and fathers, hear my defense before you now.' "**

Notice that Paul used conciliatory language by respectfully calling his persecutors "brothers and fathers." And, instead of speaking Greek, he spoke in Aramaic, the Hebrew dialect preferred by first-century Jews. Paul spoke from steps overlooking the crowd, placing himself in a position "over" his opponents. Paul was a master of the subtleties of style.

Transformation How about you? Have you learned to assess your audience and adapt your style to meet their needs? If you are preparing without considering subject, size, setting, and seniority, then you are only partially preparing. Perhaps the size, setting, and seniority will stay consistent during a particular course you are teaching. But the subject changes regularly, and like a recipe, one ingredient can affect all the others.

Make a small chart with four columns. At the top of the four columns write the four words SUBJECT, SIZE, SETTING, and SENIORITY. Under SUBJECT, list the upcoming topics you are planning to teach. Under the other three columns make notes as to how each of the subjects should be taught in light of the audience's size, setting, and seniority.

A custom designed cape honors both tailor and prince.

> **Total freedom in a speech is a speech without a strategy, and that is a speech without power.**
>
> James W. Robinson

Time for a Style Adjustment

Teacher Today, it's Pastor Douglas' turn for confession: "On one occasion, I had two speaking engagements, back-to-back. The first was in a preaching class at the seminary downtown. The second was later the same day during chapel at a Christian high school in the suburbs. 'No problem,' I figured. 'I'll just use the same message twice.'

"Well, everything went well at the seminary, but after five minutes at the Christian school the yawns and shuffles told me I should have left my professorial style at the seminary—where it belonged!

"What did I do? The only thing I could do. I changed styles pronto! I tried to teach the same material but in a completely different way. I loosened my tie, stopped worrying about getting it perfect, and moved away from the podium down into the audience.

"It worked! But it was a close call!"

Truth / Acts 23:2–5 In at least one situation, Paul switched his style dramatically—on a moment's notice. Paul was called before the Sanhedrin, the ruling council of Jewish elders, to face charges of disrupting Jerusalem with his teaching. When the high priest unlawfully ordered Paul roughed up, Paul confronted him harshly, not knowing who he was. When Paul learned he was speaking to the high priest, he immediately softened his style, employing respect and humility.

"And the high priest Ananias commanded those who stood by him to strike him [Paul] on the mouth. Then Paul said to him, 'God will strike you, you whitewashed wall!' . . . And those who stood by said, 'Do you revile God's high priest?' Then Paul said, 'I did not know, brethren, that he was the high priest; for it is written, "You shall not speak evil of a ruler of your people." ' "

Transformation Does your teaching style have enough fluidity and flexibility to respond quickly to the inevitable unexpected circumstances which arise in teaching?

For example, if you're teaching teens, and the desks seem to be full of mannequins with lifeless faces, your first thought might be—it's my material. Wrong. Your topic is contemporary music, a sure winner. Okay, it's got to be the kids. Ummm, probably not. They do this topic for hours in their free time. Okay, that leaves me. Time to adjust! Instead of reading my research paper, let's pop in a CD and listen! Oooh, they *are* alive. And they discuss, too—thanks to a style adjustment!

> Teachers use O'Toole's Law, not Murphy's. Murphy said: "If anything can go wrong, it will." O'Toole said: "Murphy was an optimist."

No change in the pulpit, no change in the pew.

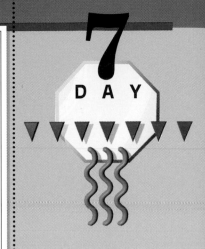

How to Improve Your Style

Teacher "I truly love to teach," Gayle says sincerely. "I am genuinely committed to the need and power of God's truth to change lives. That's why I chose a vocation in Christian education. But right now I feel totally inadequate, not to mention discouraged."

"I can tell you're a bit discouraged, Gayle, but that doesn't mean you're inadequate to teach," Carla responds. "Do you know what's behind all this?"

Gayle continues: "Well, the past few months I've had to do more actual teaching instead of just administering teachers. And I am not encouraged by what I see myself doing! I don't know if I can become a teacher with style. I feel like sticking to administration and leaving the teaching to you guys."

"Gayle, you're forgetting a cardinal rule," says Angelo: *"Great teachers are not born, and not produced on assembly lines—they are developed over time.* I've discovered that the more I understand about teaching, and the more I practice what I understand, the more my students respond—and learn!"

Truth / Philippians 4:8–9 It is always a challenge to enter a new venture—or an old one with new demands. Take the Philippian believers. They were learning to live an entirely new way. Their pagan practices were being replaced by the values of the kingdom of God—and it wasn't easy. Paul knew they needed two things: understanding and practice.

> **"Finally, brethren, whatever things are true . . . noble . . . just . . . pure . . . lovely . . . of good report, if there is any virtue and if there is anything praiseworthy—meditate on these things. The things which you learned and received and heard and saw in me, these do, and the God of peace will be with you."**

Meditating on new information produces deep understanding. Practice produces new skills. Whether you're a teacher or a believer learning to walk with the Lord, the process is the same—you are always a learner.

Transformation A helpful part of learning a new skill is a mentor—someone to imitate, from whom you can learn as you grow. In Timothy's case, there was Paul. Do you have a mentor?

Think about a teacher you really admire—one in whom character and classroom effectiveness are a seamless blend. If that person would be an appropriate mentor for you (seek your pastor's counsel if you're not sure), approach him or her and inquire about beginning a mentoring and learning relationship. With understanding and practice, you'll soon be mentoring others in teaching with style!

Don't give up! You will be tomorrow where your mentor is today.

> Diamonds are only chunks of coal that stuck to their jobs.
>
> Minnie Smith

A Moment with Max

❝ Okay, everyone, time to get down to the nitty-gritty! You've learned some great things—now it's time to put them to work.

So where do we start? Remember our instructor's last point in this session—how style is a learned skill and can be significantly improved through understanding and practice? Let's tackle that one first! Are you with me? I've given you six projects to consider—easy or hard, begin where it's best for you!

Now, I've done all these projects, and I know you can too. So let's get with it! Pretty soon, you'll be teaching with style just like me! Thrilling to imagine, isn't it? ❞

Just Beginning

1 Reflect on some of your recent classes and write down what you think your students saw and heard when you taught. Describe your teaching style: voice, movement, variety, personality traits. Keep this self-portrait handy for review at the end of this course.

2 Interview the teacher or communicator with the most effective teaching style you know. Ask about style: history of successes and failures, disciplines he or she follows, how natural weaknesses were overcome, and how you might improve your own teaching style.

3 Purchase and study at least one book on effective teaching or communication style in the next six months. Make written notes on those points most applicable to your teaching, and implement them. Develop your own library of style resources for study.

4 Plan a one-month prayer focus on your own teaching ministry. Ask God for His insight and evaluation of your present level of commitment to teach with style and effectiveness. Renew your commitments to God in writing, and keep in a safe place for future review.

Advanced

5 Submit your teaching style to your peers for evaluation and improvement. Ask one fellow-teacher per month to evaluate your teaching style. Save the written report for comparison at a later date to note changes, progress, and other areas for improvement.

6 Involve your students in your quest to teach with effective style. Devise an anonymous questionnaire which they can fill out periodically on aspects of your teaching style: your personal traits, what's exciting, what's boring, progress made. Summarize and discuss.

"Only take heed to yourself, and diligently keep yourself, lest you forget the things your eyes have seen, and lest they depart from your heart all the days of your life. And teach them to your children and your grandchildren."

Deuteronomy 4:9

"Lay the Foundation"

The person who lays a foundation to teach with style knows that **style is the process by which a teacher delivers the subject to the student.** In fact, he or she knows that style will be the **primary cause of student boredom or excitement.** This teacher agrees that the **teacher is responsible** for style—it is **within his or her complete control.** While style **is influenced by personality,** it is determined by **the role the teacher selects. Subject, size, setting, and seniority** are conscious considerations in choosing a style. Additionally, style **is fluid and must be adjusted according to the response of the audience.** Are teachers-with-style born with style? No! They develop it over time, since **style is a learned skill and can be significantly improved through understanding and practice.**

The teacher who lays the foundation is a person who Teaches with Style! By the grace of God, you can be that person!

I commit to Teach with Style through carefully laying the foundation— the foundation of universal principles which, when practiced, result in LifeChange in my students.

_____ /2-15-02
Signature/Date

BIBLICAL
CHARACTERISTICS

When God communicates, He captures everyone's attention—big or small! The characteristics of His style are easy to identify and to imitate. But you have to know what to look for—and where!

INSTRUCTION

INTRODUCTION

Many speakers exhausts audience before he exhausts his subject.

CHARACTERISTICS 1

God's style is *Memorable.*

Q: What do you do when you end class to ensure message is memorable!

The ignorance giant tries to blind us to God's style.

CHARACTERISTICS 2

God's style is *Unexpected*.

~ *Balim & his donkey*
~ *Parting of Red Sea & Jordan*

CHARACTERISTICS 3

God's style is _Visual_ (you are your best visual aid)
-- Tabernacle

Pharaoh nearly croaked when he saw God's teaching style.

CHARACTERISTICS 4

God's style is _Unique_.

CHARACTERISTICS 5

God's style is _Multi-Sensory_.

Touched
Ate with

CHARACTERISTICS 6

God's style is _Captivating_.
Daniel 5:5,6

CHARACTERISTICS 7

God's style is _Incarnational (lived among us to teach us)_.
~ Washing Feet

The most memorable part of Prof. Rimshot's talk was . . .

let's see . . . no . . . hmmm . . . maybe it was . . . no . . . hmmm . . .

What was his talk about again?

CONCLUSION

Christianity that is Biblical
Content that is

A ▷ Mastering the Minimum

A fellow teacher misses this session due to illness. He calls the next day and says, "I'm in a hurry, but tell me—bottom line—what was the instructor's message?" Write your answer:

_____

_____

_____

B ◇ A Characteristics Check-Up

Evaluate your teaching style below in light of the seven Biblical Characteristics. (Record your score in the space.)

Never	Seldom	Sometimes	Usually	Always
1	2	3	4	5

1. I take responsibility for the "memorability" of my content, not resting until I know my students have it.   (___)

2. I am comfortable using "shock" treatment with my students to convey a point or get their attention.   (___)

3. I use overhead projectors, film strips, videos, charts, graphs, maps, objects, and other visuals in my class.   (___)

4. I prepare "one-time" teaching moments for my class which I know I will not repeat since they are unique.   (___)

5. I plan learning experiences which utilize the senses of taste, touch, and smell as well as seeing and hearing.   (___)

6. I consider it a personal goal to capture my students' attention and hold it from the beginning to the end of class. (___)

7. I feel confident that I am a "living lecture" for my students; that my life illustrates the truths I teach.   (___)

Add up your total points and enter your score in the margin.

"God is pretty stylish in the way He communicates, don't you think? Time now to take a look at *your* style. Don't worry—this grade will not become a part of your permanent record!"

My score: [____]

30 – 35 Expert: making characteristics a priority!

25 – 29 Advanced: your students appreciate you!

20 – 24 Intermediate: could go either way!

15 – 19 Beginner: unclear on the concept!

10 – 14 Boring: what was the question?

C ▶ A Captivating Characteristic

Jesus Christ is acknowledged by almost everyone to be the most captivating and effective teacher who ever lived. From your recollection of His ministry, what made His teaching style so captivating? *Spoke w/authority*
Spoke w/ Compassion

Who is the most captivating teacher you have ever heard? Compare his or her style to that of Jesus. What techniques did he or she use that were similar, or different? What kept you captivated?

Dr. Tony Evans - Teaching was relational

> " All right! I can tell you're ready for more! How about a week's worth? Just ahead are seven daily readings in Style which reveal more about the Biblical characteristics. You're fast becoming an expert in this, you know. To be honest, I can use the company. It gets a little lonely at the top! "

D ◆ What Are Your Characteristics?

If your students thoroughly understood the seven Biblical Characteristics, they would choose number _____ as being the characteristic most evident in your life.

They would choose number _____ as the one needing the most improvement.

Try to recall a student conversation or incident which led you to answer as you did above:

E ◆ Make Your Characteristics Biblical!

What two things can you do in the immediate future to impact the area you cited for improvement in D above?

1. _____

2. _____

God's Style is Memorable

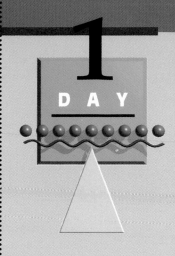

Teacher As a science teacher, Angelo Perez has learned a very important lesson: The more effort he puts into making content memorable, the more his students remember!

"Imagine what my science class would be like if I just stood at the front of the class reading and never did an experiment," Angelo says. "Sure, I could still give my students plenty of content. I could lecture about how certain chemicals respond when combined, or I could teach detailed information about the anatomy of mammals.

"But I've noticed that when I take time to create an emotional memory *in* class, or give the students a memory device to help them retain the material *after* class—they've got it. Like the time we dissected frogs, then sampled frog legs as a delicacy! A student from last year's class wanted to be my assistant this year just so she could watch two of her friends have this 'delectable' experience. She had not forgotten!"

Truth / 1 Corinthians 11:23b-25 Most teacher training programs devote little time to showing teachers how to help students remember. But in the Bible, we see that God devotes significant effort to driving His truth into the memories of His people.

On the night before Jesus' death, He instituted a tangible memorial of the work He was about to do on the cross.

> **"The Lord Jesus on the same night in which He was betrayed took bread; and when He had given thanks, He broke it and said, 'Take, eat; this is My body which is broken for you; do this in remembrance of Me.' In the same manner, He also took the cup after supper, saying, 'This cup is the new covenant in My blood. This do, as often as you drink it, in remembrance of Me.' "**

After 2000 years, Christians still use the bread and the cup to remember Him—and what He taught.

Transformation Jesus associated the events surrounding His death with concrete objects—bread and wine. Review your own memories of your childhood and the recent past. Why do you remember what you remember? Sights and sounds, feelings and facts, rhymes and repetition. They all contribute, don't they?

These factors can also contribute to your students' retention of your lesson content as well. Pray right now that God will let you see your students as family for whom you want memories to be precious and plentiful.

Material made memorable means material made livable.

> ▶ **For the next seven days, explore how God's style can be found in Scripture and applied in the classroom!**

2
DAY

God's Style is Unexpected

Teacher "Then, instead of ending the story as they expected me to, I jumped up and shouted that the wolf leaped over the boiling pot and ate up all three little pigs! Suddenly the whole class of second-graders sat straight up—'No!' they shouted, 'That's not the way it ends!' "

Carla Mattland is recounting an experience she had with her second-graders that day. And the lesson she is relating is indispensable:

"These kids have heard this story countless times. They knew what to expect and when to expect it. A lot of them were 'drifting.' But when I surprised them with the unexpected ending, they came alive.

"So many things in life are predictable," Carla continues. "And the predictable is often boring. When we know what to expect, we fall asleep mentally. A surprise—something unexpected—rivets our attention and renews our interest."

Truth / Numbers 22:28 God understands the powerful effect of surprise. When He wanted Balaam to speak a message of blessing about the children of Israel, rather than a message of cursing, He focused Balaam's attention instantaneously with a talking donkey!

"The LORD opened the mouth of the donkey, and she said to Balaam, 'What have I done to you, that you have struck me these three times?' "

After getting Balaam's attention, God shocked him again with an astonishing vision: "Then the LORD opened Balaam's eyes, and he saw the Angel of the LORD standing in the way with His drawn sword in His hand; and he bowed his head and fell flat on his face" (Numbers 22:31).

Balaam got God's point, and repented in a hurry!

Transformation Let's fine tune our understanding and definition of "unexpected." It's not just surprise. The notion of the unexpected in teaching with style goes beyond surprise to the level of "shock." Not a "scary" shock, mind you, but an arresting one.

You can be surprised by something with which you are totally familiar but which you weren't actually expecting. In that sense, unexpected equals surprise. In this case, how many times had Balaam seen a talking donkey? Zero! Therefore, what God did SHOCKED Balaam. His senses were called to immediate attention! His breath was taken away! He was one focused prophet—ready to learn! That is what we mean by unexpected.

And that's the effect your style can have as well. Try something unexpected in class—and get ready for some shocking results!

> **Often times, what students need is a bit of "shock therapy."**

> Whoever can surprise well must conquer.
>
> John Paul Jones

God's Style is Visual

Teacher Steven Kirby feels as though he's getting into a rut with his business luncheon and Bible study.

"It seems the material just isn't clicking. Folks seem a bit bored."

"Do you use handouts in your study, Steven?" Carla asks.

"Sure," Steven says, "all the time. In fact, I give them an outline of the material I cover every week."

Carla asks another pointed question: "Would you give an outline to someone with whom you were trying to do business?"

"Goodness, no!" Steven says. "The proposals we send to prospects have charts, graphs, slides, and the like. Without the visuals we would fail to communicate our message to the client."

The group was silent for a moment as the "Aha" began to dawn on Steven.

"Have I just been impaled on the point of my own practice?" Steven asked meekly. The group laughed with Steven, delivering the answer: Yes!

Truth / Revelation 19:11-13 In our high-tech, media bombarded world, teaching with style must be a visual enterprise! God understands that. His Gospel has the power to change lives and cultures. But first it has to get a hearing— or maybe a "viewing."

When God wanted the Apostle John to understand the nature of Christ's return, He didn't only deliver a set of facts or propositions. Instead, He used visual aids along with facts. He *showed* John a vision of Christ as King, riding a white horse to victory over Satan's followers.

> **"Then I saw heaven opened, and behold, a white horse. And He who sat on him was called Faithful and True, and in righteousness He judges and makes war. His eyes were like a flame of fire, and on His head were many crowns. He had a name written that no one knew except Himself. He was clothed with a robe dipped in blood, and His name is called The Word of God."**

Transformation The next time you are watching television, listening to a sermon in church, or having a conversation with a friend, close your eyes. Even right now, close your eyes for a moment. After opening them, think of what you've missed: colors, expressions, shapes— the whole realm of visual stimuli. Now think of your students going through their educational process with their eyes closed. Pretty discouraging!

When we teach without using visuals, the effect is the same. Except in the classroom it's not called discouraging—it's called boring!

Due to rising inflation, a picture is now worth a million words.

> ▶ Conserve energy when you teach. Substitute one picture for every thousand words!

God's Style is Unique

Teacher "Last night, I went to observe a youth group that has been having a big impact in youth ministry circles," Gayle Henson says, shaking her head and laughing. "You won't believe what that youth pastor did.

"A couple of weeks earlier, he had promised his kids that if 90 percent of them scored a perfect 100 on a Bible basics test, he would drink the grossest drink the students could create in a blender. This was a one-time, unique motivational tool, he had said. If less than 90 percent scored 100, he wouldn't drink it and he wouldn't repeat the offer.

"I'm sure you can guess what happened. Ninety-seven percent of the group scored perfectly—and it was a tough quiz! Before my eyes, he drank a concoction of . . . well, trust me—it was awful! No, it was worse than awful! Anyway, the kids loved it! They went wild, and learned! And he survived!"

Truth / Matthew 14:25, 28-31 To teach the disciples the extent of His power and the power of faith, Jesus did something unique, something nobody else had ever done or could ever do.

While the disciples were in a boat in the middle of the Sea of Galilee, Jesus approached them by walking on the water—and called Peter to come to Him by walking on the water as well! Jesus orchestrated this teaching event as a one-time demonstration, never to be repeated—or forgotten!

"Now in the fourth watch of the night Jesus went to them, walking on the sea . . . . And Peter answered Him and said, 'Lord, if it is You, command me to come to You on the water.' So He said, 'Come.' And when Peter had come down out of the boat, he walked on the water to go to Jesus . . . . And beginning to sink he cried out, saying, 'Lord, save me!' And immediately Jesus stretched out His hand and caught him, and said to him, 'O you of little faith, why did you doubt?' "

Transformation Synonyms for the word *unique* are *incomparable, matchless, unparalleled, unrivaled, sole,* and *only.*

Questions: How many times do we include something in our teaching that our students will never forget because it was unparalleled or unrivaled? Do we demonstrate love for our students by orchestrating a unique event for them—*just for them*—which they will always remember? How long do you think Peter remembered the lesson from the Sea of Galilee?

Final question: Will you plan a unique learning experience this week?

You and your students are unique. What about your lessons?

What you must dare is to be yourself.

Dag Hammarskjold

God's Style is Multisensory

Teacher "Unfortunately, not everyone can do this," Denise Farris says, "but one thing that helped my Bible study understand the Scriptures in a new way was to take a trip to Israel together. The Word of God simply came alive.

"In Israel we had an incredible sense of learning from life itself. We realized that Jesus used everything around Him when He taught. Everyday objects and customs—even the culture, geography, and politics—were teaching tools. Every one of the five senses were used as learning channels for His disciples. He touched, spoke, showed, fed, and even made a significant spiritual point using a costly, aromatic perfume!

"Since then, I've tried to open all the senses of my students—it works!"

Truth / Isaiah 6:1-4, 6-7 God's teaching methods aren't limited only to the spoken word. God communicates through all the senses to the whole person.

When God called the Prophet Isaiah to deliver a message of judgment to the Israelites, He engaged all of Isaiah's senses. God's glory invaded Isaiah through sight, sound, aroma, and touch; his mind could not escape the message.

> "I saw the Lord sitting on a throne, high and lifted up, and the train of His robe filled the temple. Above it stood seraphim . . . . And one cried to another and said: 'Holy, holy, holy is the LORD of hosts; the whole earth is full of His glory!' And the posts of the door were shaken by the voice of him who cried out, and the house was filled with smoke . . . . Then one of the seraphim flew to me, having in his hand a live coal which he had taken with the tongs from the altar. And he touched my mouth with it, and said: 'Behold, this has touched your lips; your iniquity is taken away . . . .' "

Transformation Some of your most lifechanging experiences have probably come in informal settings where an unexpected situation engulfed you from every direction. Learning is mandatory—and usually multisensory—when that happens!

Unfortunately, the more traditional and structured our teaching, the less multisensory it is; the more spontaneous, the more multisensory. Jesus never said, "Let's have a class." Rather, our world was His classroom. He took advantage of every situation—and all the senses. You can do the same!

Multiply: 5 senses x the number of your students = multisensory!

> If you had five hands with which to work, would you use only two? Why then do we teach to only two senses when our students have five?

God's Style is Captivating

Teacher "Speaking of youth ministry," Pastor Douglas adds, "we tried something with our high schoolers recently that I believe had a lifechanging impact. I have never seen them so captivated."

"Well, you've captivated me. Tell us what you did!" pleaded Carla.

"We don't suspect any of our young people in the recent rash of break-ins around town, but I wanted to capture their attention quickly about the folly of such behavior. So we took the entire high school youth group to the state prison where they met with some convicted burglars.

"You could have heard a pin drop as some of the inmates shared how they entered a life of crime at a young age and ended up in prison. Our kids were visibly moved—even shaken and scared—beyond my expectations! I doubt if any one of them will entertain the thought of stealing anything!"

Truth / Exodus 3:2-3 God's style is captivating. He does astonishing things, awesome things, to communicate His message.

In Egypt, Moses was a wealthy, highly trained, and educated prince living as Pharaoh's grandson. As a privileged member of the royal household, there was little that Moses had not seen or done. When it came time for Moses to serve God, how would God get and keep Moses' attention? He had to create an experience which was new to Moses—a teaching method unseen in his lifetime.

"The Angel of the LORD appeared to [Moses] in a flame of fire from the midst of a bush. So he looked, and behold, the bush burned with fire, but the bush was not consumed. Then Moses said, 'I will now turn aside and see this great sight, why the bush does not burn.' "

Once God captured and held Moses' attention, He spoke. Moses' eventual success for the Lord began with the impact of that initial moment.

Transformation Look carefully at the word *captivate*. Do you see a familiar root term there? Yes—at the heart of *captivate* is *capture*. It is very difficult for a person who is captured to escape.

Apply this concept to your teaching. When your class is captivated, they will find it almost impossible to escape your content. You have erected an invisible wall around them which prevents their minds from wandering. So completely have you piqued their interest, even their curiosity, that they have committed themselves totally to you in that moment.

Isn't this how God works with us? Captivated by His love, we dare not wander off! Capture your students with creative teaching style—this week!

> **Use style to turn your class into a captive audience.**

To be held captive by love and fascination is to be the most fortunate of captives.

God's Style is Incarnational

Teacher "I admit it. I'm a perfectionist," Liz Darby tells the others. "If a teacher explained some aspect of the spiritual life, my first response was to ask: 'How? Why? Can you explain it better?' I used to drive teachers crazy asking questions they couldn't answer. Unfortunately, much spiritual truth defies easy explanation and pat answers.

"It was not until I was in a class taught by a godly Christian woman that something clicked. She not only taught us the truth, she lived it. I spent time with her, visited in her home, even went on some trips with her. Her life actually answered more questions than her lectures.

"She taught me that truth incarnated is really more powerful than truth explained. And guess what other Master Teacher used the method of incarnation as the basis of His ministry? I think my teacher was in pretty good company, don't you?"

Truth / John 1:1, 14 Isn't it amazing that when God decided to teach the human race about His love and salvation, He "incarnated" Himself? He became exactly what He wanted humankind to become. So there would be no doubt about the meaning of His words, He lived out the definition daily.

> **"In the beginning was the Word, and the Word was with God, and the Word was God. . . . And the Word became flesh and dwelt among us, and we beheld His glory, the glory as of the only begotten of the Father, full of grace and truth."**

Think of it—"the Word became flesh and dwelt among us." As a human being, Jesus taught as do most teachers—with words. But He Himself was actually a word—*the* Word—which He both spoke and lived.

Transformation Here's an even more sobering thought. How do our lives measure up to our words? As Christian teachers, do we emulate the model of Christ who *was* what He taught? A model is the most powerful teaching tool available. Teachers must learn to be living lectures to their students.

What do you teach? Algebra, history, English, the Bible, a skills class? Regardless of your content, there is a way to incarnate your teaching. Whatever you expect your students to do or be as a result of your teaching, you must do and be it for them. You will have no more powerful impact on your students than the impact of your life.

God can show you the way—after all, incarnation is His idea!

> **Truth taught, reinforced by truth lived, is difficult, if not impossible, to ignore.**

Serve your students some "content con carne."

A Moment with Max

" Okay—we've heard the message on Biblical characteristics of style, been through the interaction topics, done our seven daily devotions—and did it all with style, I might add! Way to go! Now it's time for a little homework. But don't worry—this is FUN homework, because your students will end up loving you! We're going to focus on the second point: God's style is unexpected. These projects will help you do some unexpected things with YOUR students. Boy, will they ever be surprised! So will you—at the results! Okay—check out the projects. Find the one or two most suited to where you are, and do something

UNEXPECTED."

Just Beginning

1 Surprise your class by cancelling all scheduled activity for the day. Devote the time to your students: how they're doing, how they're feeling, what their concerns are in relation to class. Perhaps bring some refreshments to class for all to enjoy.

2 Give your students a copy of the next quiz or test you have planned. Tell them you want them all to make a "100"—that you're telling them now what they'll need to know to score perfectly. They'll be shocked, since most teachers want students to *guess* what's on the test!

3 **Create** an environment for learning by experience and identification. For instance, have the class wear blindfolds for half the day to experience the challenges of living as a blind person. Have them fast at lunch to understand hunger.

4 **Bring** to class facts, pictures, videos, music, magazines, and other supportive materials to shock your students with the reality of your content. Overwhelm them with data to drive home the point.

5 **Bring** in a person who can deliver a dramatic rebuke to the class in an area of complacency: a law enforcement officer, a convict, a substance abuser. Have them speak firmly to the class in order to create a shock effect. Be sure to relieve any "pressure" that is created.

6 **Reveal** some aspect of your own life or background (or that of a well-known person whose background is public knowledge) unknown to the class which might surprise them. Do this carefully and appropriately, making the shock value support the point of the lesson.

God, who at various times and in different ways spoke in time past to the fathers by the prophets, has in these last days spoken to us by His Son . . . .

Hebrews 1:1-2

"Know the Scriptures"

The person who knows the Scriptures is a person who is becoming equipped to teach with style. When the teacher with God's style teaches, he or she will be remembered, since God's style is **memorable**. It is also **unexpected**—at times shocking students into a state of attentiveness—much as God did at times. God shocked not only by His words, but by His actions, since His style was not only verbal but **visual**. His style was anything but commonplace—it was often **unique**, only for one particular audience. Having captured their students' attention, teachers with style stretch them by making content **multisensory**. Teachers with style keep students' attention by being **captivating**. And they model content by being **incarnational**—showing as well as telling.

The person who knows the Scriptures is a person who Teaches with Style! By the grace of God, you can be that person!

I commit to Teach with Style through a growing knowledge of the Scriptures—that lifetime acquisition of the knowledge of God and His style, which, when practiced, results in LifeChange in my students.

Signature/Date

INTERNAL BELIEFS

Teaching with style doesn't just happen. Style is the overflow of a heart burning with the basics— the basics which form the basis of style. Do you know what they are? You're about to discover them for yourself!

INSTRUCTION

INTRODUCTION

Mr. Indifference; Makes you comfortable, cold in heart.
Ezra 7:10 ..... prepared his heart, ... do it & teach it ...
- We must be passionate about communicating.
- Minister should go to each service as if it's his first, best, last.
- Poke the fire, stir up the gift.

BELIEF 1

Passion to *Communicate*.

"I like to see a
man preach as
if he were
fighting bees."

Abraham Lincoln

BELIEF 2

Love for *Students*
Many love preaching, but not students.

1 CORN 13:1
1 Peter 4:8
Mark 6:34

BELIEF 3

Sense of commission from _God_.

Matt 28:19
2 Tim 2:2
Deut 6:7
Titus 2:3:4

BELIEF 4

High degree of _Preparation_.

1. _Personal_
2. _Presentation_
3. _People_
4. _Place_ (Pray prior to arrival of students)
2 Tim 2 8:15a
1 Tim 4:15

Rhonda Relay hits the ground running when it comes to lesson preparation.

BELIEF 5

Conviction of the message's

Power
Become incarnational — 1 Peter 4:11
· God changing our lives

Mr. N.A. Fog's
message went up
in smoke.

BELIEF 6

Integrity with the *Message*
My worth to God in public is what I am in private.

_____

_____

BELIEF 7

Dependence upon *God* .

Eph 5:18
Eph 3:28
2 CORN 3:5,6

God the Father   *Secrets of Supernatural Style*
                        Son   *Spirit*
Creativity   *Incarnated*   *Inspires*

Isaiah 6:5-8

CONCLUSION

_____

_____

_____

_____

_____

A · Mastering the Minimum

You've just returned home from Session Three. You record in your journal what you felt was the primary message of this session for any teacher. You enter today's date and write . . .

_____

_____

_____

B · Focusing on <u>Your</u> Internal Beliefs

Evaluate your teaching style below in light of the seven Internal Beliefs. (Record your score in the space.)

Never	Seldom	Sometimes	Usually	Always
1	2	3	4	5

1. On any given day, those who observe me would quickly agree that teaching is my consuming passion. (_____)

2. I develop close relationships and friendships among my students which go beyond class time. (_____)

3. Whenever I teach, it is with a sense of purpose that God *wants* me to teach, that it is His will for me to do so. (_____)

4. I arrive at my class time refreshed, confident, and well-versed having prepared my lessons in advance. (_____)

5. Regardless of what content I teach, I am totally committed to the lifechanging potential of my lesson. (_____)

6. My conscience remains clear as I teach because I practice the content I am communicating to others. (_____)

7. I have a clear and practical understanding of how dependence upon God impacts the lesson I present. (_____)

Add up your total points and enter your score in the margin.

INTERACTION

" Are you getting more comfortable with Teaching with Style? This session is really the 'heart' of the matter. So let's dive in and share some insights and—oh yes, a little quiz! **"**

My score: [   ]

30 – 35 Expert: making beliefs a priority!

25 – 29 Advanced: your students appreciate you!

20 – 24 Intermediate: could go either way!

15 – 19 Beginner: unclear on the concept!

10 – 14 Boring: what was the question?

C A Barometer for Internal Beliefs

Internally, what is the difference between a teacher who is "recruited" vs. one who senses a "commission" from God to teach? What impact does one's internal sense of settledness and mission have on the way one teaches? Complete the sentences below:

I have known teachers who were recruited to teach because they were "available." I would describe their teaching as . . .

Mediocre

I have known other teachers who *know,* from the Lord, they are to teach their class. I would describe their teaching as . . .

Mediocre = middle of the mountain: Inspiring

Kill the giant of ind: Psalm 139:23,24 Pervade with passion.

D Broadcasting Your Beliefs

If your students thoroughly understood the seven Internal Beliefs, they would choose number _____ as being the belief most evident in your life.

They would choose number _____ as the one needing the most improvement.

Try to recall a student conversation or incident which led you to answer as you did above:

_____

E Becoming a Belief-er

In the area you cited for improvement in D above, write down two steps you can take this week to make progress:

1. _____

2. _____

"The Internal Beliefs just feel right, don't they? I know they do for me. When I practice the beliefs, I know I'm being the kind of teacher God created me to be. Let's push ahead now to His Word for some daily insight into the seven Internal Beliefs!"

Passion to Communicate

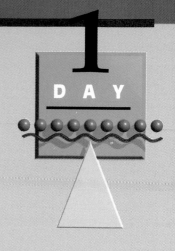

Teacher Angelo Perez is experiencing dangerous symptoms. "You know," Angelo says in a thinking-out-loud manner, "when I first started teaching I didn't know the meaning of 'mediocrity.' I was fired up! I had the proverbial 'fire in the belly' about teaching! But lately, my passion to teach has been deflating like a slow leak in a tire. My problem isn't finding the leak—it's getting motivated enough to look for it!

"My original vision of teaching was like a kaleidoscope—bright colors, beautiful patterns, always new and different! But now I feel like I'm flying blind into a cloud bank every time I walk into class. What do I do?"

Truth / 2 Timothy 1:6 Any endeavor, including teaching, will lose its excitement if it's not nurtured. The Apostle Paul understood this—and was concerned that his protégé Timothy not grow cold.

"Therefore I remind you to stir up the gift of God which is in you through the laying on of my hands."

As long as Timothy was in Paul's presence, he was motivated. But when Paul sent Timothy to Ephesus, he was on his own. Timothy was like a coal removed from the fire—in danger of failing if not fanned. In fact, the words *stir up* here mean to continuously fan the coal—keep it ablaze, rekindle it.

But whose job is that? Let's paraphrase what Paul was saying: "Timothy, you are a living coal. You must continuously rekindle and refuel yourself so that you burn brightly—else you will lose your fire for Christ. You are at once the fuel, the fire, and the fan. No one else will do this for you. You must do it for yourself!"

Transformation Those are strong words from a strong teacher, but Paul spoke from experience. As the apostolic missionary, who was there to keep him motivated? Often, no one. Paul had learned that he alone was responsible for keeping alive in himself the passion for his work (see 2 Corinthians 6 and 11).

Have you developed the skill of fanning your own flame? Has it become a habit? If not, you can begin now to stir up the fire in your heart.

One way to prepare for class is to do something highly motivating just before you teach. Do you love inspirational music? Majestic oratory? Does a time of prayer with the Lord help you refocus? Perhaps reading about famous heroes—even martyrs!—is your key. Identify and practice the most motivating thing you can before you teach.

Whatever fans your flame, start to use it now. When you begin to see the coal glow, you'll know that the flame of enthusiasm is close behind!

▶ **Use the next seven days to establish a Biblical foundation for your internal beliefs.**

Don't forget: teachers with style are fired up, not burned out.

2

DAY

Love for Students

Teacher "Gayle. Hey Gayle. Oh, Gay-y-y-y-le!" Carla laughs as she brings Gayle back to reality from staring into space.

Gayle is preoccupied—and it shows. She's had listless days and restless nights. The reason? She's feeling the pain of a guilty conscience.

"Sorry—I was thinking about my junior high students," Gayle says with a hint of anger in her voice. "Sometimes they drive me crazy! I think I've lost whatever love for them I ever had. I've been teaching Sunday school in different capacities for 15 years, but I don't ever remember feeling this way. I have to admit it: I just can't stand a few of these wild junior-highers. And frankly, I feel guilty because of it."

Truth / 1 Corinthians 13:1-2 Gayle is allowing her heart to become embittered—a hard pattern to break. If she is to change her attitude about her students (as well as regain her peace of mind and heart), she needs a healthy serving of repentance in light of 1 Corinthians 13.

"Though I speak with the tongues of men and of angels, but have not love, I have become as sounding brass or a clanging cymbal. And though I have the gift of prophecy, and understand all mysteries and all knowledge, and though I have all faith, so that I could remove mountains, but have not love, I am nothing."

God is love, and He calls us to serve Him and others in love. If we show no love to our students, we negate the power of the gift God has given. Without love, Christian education isn't Christlike. It's "Christian" in name only.

Transformation Here are two strategies for replacing anger or frustration with genuine love and concern for your students:

First, identify the students God has given you to develop your heart of love, and pray for them by name. Make sure you pray for them every day, and note the changes you see—in them *and* yourself.

Second, serve them. Visit their homes. Take them out for pizza. Get inside their hearts and minds to see what makes them tick. In serving their needs, you will change, and you'll likely gain insight into their behavior. Perhaps circumstances at home, low self-esteem, or other problems are at the root of their unruly behavior.

Prayer and service are the Christian's secret weapons. But love is the stone that hones those weapons. Pray first for yourself, then your students. Love begins on your knees and flows through your words and actions.

> **We do not teach math, history, science, or grammar— we teach students.**

Knowing you care precedes caring about what you know.

Sense of Commission from God

Teacher Denise Farris is late. Considering the way her last Sunday school class went, she almost stayed home. But somehow she sensed that she couldn't miss tonight's meeting. She tiptoes into the room and quickly sits down, saying nothing.

"Hi, Denise!" a cheerful voice calls out. Denise glances up and sees Carla smiling at her. "I'm really glad you made it. Tonight is going to be a real encouragement to all of us."

"I hope so," Denise says softly. "One thing I need right now is encouragement. To be honest, Carla, I'm thinking about telling my pastor I'm not going to teach Sunday school anymore. I just don't think I'm cut out to teach. I don't even know if God's *called* me to teach. Maybe only people with that spiritual gift should be doing the teaching. What do you think?"

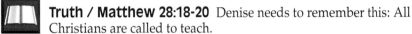

Truth / Matthew 28:18-20 Denise needs to remember this: All Christians are called to teach.

Of course, not all believers have the same teaching abilities. Nor are all Christians equally endowed with the spiritual gift of teaching. But every person who has trusted Christ can obey His words:

> **"Then Jesus came and spoke to them, saying, 'All authority has been given to Me in heaven and on earth. Go therefore and make disciples of all the nations, baptizing them in the name of the Father and of the Son and of the Holy Spirit, teaching them to observe all things that I have commanded you; and lo, I am with you always, even to the end of the age.' "**

In His Great Commission, Christ commands all Christians to be disciple-makers. To obey His command, we must communicate truth in an understandable way—that is, every Christian must be an effective teacher. It is part of His Commission, and our job description!

Transformation If you are a Christian, you are called to teach. And to some degree, you are gifted to know and communicate His truth. That's great news! That means you can rest in His will, confidently expecting Him to empower you to fulfill His Great Commission.

Do you still have doubts? Since this is fundamentally a matter of faith—believing He wants you to teach for Him—perhaps you can settle this issue in prayer right now: *"Father, You have given me a commission: teaching Your truth. Confirm in my heart this call You have given to every believer. Help me to accept Your call and rely on Your power."*

> ▶ **The pros do the basics well every day.**
>
> **Vince Lombardi**

Accepting Christ's Great Commission is accepting a call to teach.

4 DAY

> There is one activity most likely to change the human heart: meditating on the truths of the Word of God.

High Degree of Preparation

Teacher Steven Kirby vents a mild frustration as the meeting begins: "I had to pass up a great—and I mean *great*—social opportunity a couple of nights ago to prepare for the lunchtime Bible study I lead. And to tell you the truth, I was really sorry I did.

"The party I missed would have been a great opportunity to develop a more personal relationship with the vice president from headquarters who is over my division. He was there, and I heard he was really friendly.

"And as for the Bible study, my diligent preparation didn't seem to make much difference anyway. I mean, is preparation that important? I think most of the people come for the fellowship, not the teaching. I may just 'wing it' next time and not miss out on the party. Do you guys ever think you're wasting your time with a lot of preparation?"

Truth / James 3:1 Steven needs to read and think about James' exhortation to teachers:

"My brethren, let not many of you become teachers, knowing that we shall receive a stricter judgment."

Because teaching is a speaking task, and speaking carries great potential for sin (see Proverbs 10:19), we must speak carefully as well as truthfully. Preparation is first and foremost a safeguard against leading others astray.

The Apostle Paul was an instrument of God for giving us the Scriptures. When he was writing Scripture, the Holy Spirit led his thoughts and words in such a way as to prevent him from writing anything but truth. Yet Paul didn't ignore his own preparation. Even when he was in prison, he asked his disciple Timothy to bring scrolls to him. He never stopped studying God's Word. He never stopped preparing for a new opportunity to teach.

Transformation Here's some advice for upgrading your preparation, and your *perspective* on preparation:

First, commit to God that you will take your preparation time more seriously—that it is *His* time to teach you!

Second, don't put off your preparation time to the last minute. Instead of preparing three hours the night before you teach, spread your preparation over three nights. One hour a night is a lot easier—and a lot more productive—than late-night cramming.

Third, have a friend sit in on your class and evaluate your content. Ask him or her to answer questions like these: Do I sound well-prepared? Is my information accurate? What important aspects of the subject am I overlooking? Are there areas in need of improvement?

An unprepared teacher produces unprepared students.

Conviction of the Message's Power

 Teacher "I had a fascinating experience today that I'd like to share with you," Richard Douglas says to the group. "I think it's going to encourage you and increase your confidence—at least it did mine!

"One of my church members is a very articulate young career woman. Before class she asked what I thought God would say to her if she could ask Him, face-to-face, His advice on a particular problem she has—and then she divulged the nature of her questions.

"It so happens that my lesson for that class was dealing with her exact problem. All I had to do was take her through the Scriptures I had prepared for my lesson! I answered her question from the Bible with God's own words. I knew that my answer was true for her life because it came from Scripture. I also knew God was really using me in her life—it was exciting! It dawned on me in a new way that night that when I say what God says, my speaking takes on a whole new level of power. And my confidence level in teaching, or counseling—or whatever I'm doing—goes sky-high!"

Truth / 1 Peter 4:11a The Apostle Peter holds teachers to a high standard of truth:

"If anyone speaks, let him speak as the oracles of God."

That doesn't just apply to teachers of the Bible. God reveals Himself through His Word and His world. Therefore, true statements about our experience will not contradict the truths we find in the Bible. Conversely, statements that directly contradict the Bible simply are not true.

Everything that is "true truth" is God's truth. And nothing that is untrue comes from God. If we are speaking the truth—regardless of the subject we're teaching—then we are teaching God's message on that subject, and may speak with the same confidence with which He speaks.

Transformation When was the last time you "argued"—or at least debated energetically? Did you speak forcefully, with great conviction? Of course you did! Why? Because you were convinced that your perspective was the right one. That is, you were convinced you held THE TRUTH, and the other person didn't. Was your mission to convince him and change his mind—and probably his behavior, too?

Do you teach with less conviction than you argue or debate? If you're like most people, you're a chili pepper when you argue and a vanilla bean when you teach. The truth is, you are presenting God's truth for Him, and He wants you to change people's minds! The question is, do you want the same thing He does—and as much?

> **God, Who is truth, lives in and speaks through His children.**

> **Forsake trying to communicate things that you do not feel passionate about.**
>
> James Gabor

Integrity with the Message

Teacher "I was incredibly embarrassed," Liz Darby says, shaking her head and looking at the floor. "Embarrassed and ashamed.

"After my Bible study, a young woman came up and asked me to explain in more detail how the evening's lesson worked in my personal life. And you know, I was caught. In reality, I don't know much about the subject, and I don't really practice it in my daily life at all.

"But that's not the worst of it. At that moment, I was faced with a choice. Either I could fake it, pretending to know what I was talking about, or I could confess the truth. I was faced with an integrity test—and I failed."

Truth / Galatians 1:10 The Apostle Paul strongly rebuked Christians who substituted the approval of men for obedience to Christ. Paul's concern centered on integrity:

> "Do I now persuade men, or God? Or do I seek to please men? For if I still pleased men, I would not be a servant of Christ."

Many of the Galatian Christians had begun to observe certain Jewish rituals. Their motivation? To impress some of the Jewish believers! Even Peter was guilty. Though he knew the Old Testament laws separating Jews from Gentiles were no longer in force, Peter would not eat with Gentiles when Jewish believers were present. That inconsistency made Paul angry—and with good reason!

You can study Paul's strong reaction in Galatians 2:11-16. In a confrontation between church leaders rare in Scripture, Paul challenges Peter "before them all." Integrity was a serious matter to Paul.

His point? *If you are going to teach that we are one in Christ and as true believers stand equal before Him, then you'd better live like it as well!*

Transformation The key word in today's lesson is *integrity*. Teaching with integrity means practicing what you preach—and admitting it when you fall short.

Here are some concrete ways to demonstrate integrity in your teaching:

• Plan your teaching calendar well in advance. Review upcoming subjects. Make sure your life validates the truth of what you will teach.

• If you must teach content with which you are struggling or unfamiliar, tell your class. They will understand—and they will respect your honesty.

• If you have treated your subject—or your students—without integrity, confess it as sin to God, as well as to the people you have affected.

• Finally, ask a fellow teacher to hold you accountable in this area.

Integrity is the wineskin preserving the wine of truth.

> Who dares to teach must never cease to learn.
>
> John C. Dana

Dependence Upon God

Teacher "OK, gang," Carla says to her friends. "Now it's my turn. My problem is really subtle—and therefore really challenging.

"I've been teaching children in Christian school for seven years. When I started, I was a typical rookie—scared. But I knew God was able. If I imagined some troublesome scenario on the way to work, I would pray about it immediately!

"In those days, I depended on the Lord to do in and for me what I knew I couldn't do myself. As I've gained more ability and confidence over the years, I've become a much better teacher. But I fear I've also lost the feeling—and the lifestyle—of dependence on the Lord.

"It's hard to keep my confidence and skills as a teacher from becoming 'Carla-confident' instead of 'Christ-confident.' Any ideas?"

Truth / Galatians 3:3 When the Apostle Paul encountered believers who had traded their dependence on the Lord for works done in their own strength, he asked a very pointed question:

"Are you so foolish? Having begun in the Spirit, are you now being made perfect by the flesh?"

After coming to the Lord, new Christians in Galatia were like all new believers—lots of enthusiasm and very little knowledge. But what they knew was very important: They knew they were sinners who needed God's grace and strength to live.

As they grew in their faith, however, they made a predictable mistake. They tried to produce spiritual reality by their own design instead of by depending on the Spirit. Even though they began a relationship with God apart from their own works, they were trying to continue the relationship with their works. Whatever their motivation, Paul called them "foolish" for having begun in the Spirit and trying to continue in the flesh.

Transformation In our own strength, we can never consistently accomplish anything God regards as truly good. Without the power of the indwelling Holy Spirit, our efforts to do good will ultimately fail, regardless of our increasing professional competence.

Right now, let God know in prayer of your desire to depend upon Him while you grow in ability and confidence. When you recognize that your growth is a gift from Him, you'll replace self-confidence with God-confidence!

Confess openly to the Lord in a prayer as class begins that you depend on Him—totally. Your prayer will empower you and instruct your students. Your life will be a living lesson in depending on the Spirit's power.

> **Obstacles always show up when you take your eyes off the goal.**
>
> **Pubilius Syrus**

Apart from Christ, even the best teacher can do nothing.

APPLICATION

A Moment with Max

" Here we are again, at the projects page—my favorite part of this course! Hey, I'm a hands-on kind of guy, okay? I love to learn and then make it happen! I know you love results, too! Now that we're committed to results, let's produce some!

I've found that our fourth point, High Degree of Preparation, is a good place to see some tangible things happen in a hurry. So let's work on that point first.

You know how the projects work by now, so grab a friend, pick a couple of projects, and let's get in the

HANDS-ON Mode!"

Just Beginning

1 Plan to arrive at your teaching setting a half-hour early. Pray for particular students and their needs as you walk around the room. Pray that the Holy Spirit would protect the class from any kind of disruption and anoint it for lifechange.

2 Purchase several popular secular magazines written for your class' age or interest group. Pick out quotes, pictures, facts, interviews, or other items which you could use in your class to stimulate discussion and to compare with the Bible's perspective.

ope that you'r

!

Love,
Cathy
Bonnie
Gary

3 Call 3-5 students and tell them what your topic is for the next class. Ask for their suggestions, insights, and opinions and build their responses into your preparation. Consider having a student(s) participate in the class presentation with their own contribution.

4 Identify a week in advance the Scripture passages for your upcoming class content. Meditate on those Scriptures daily. Ask God to give you insights, illustrations, confirmations, and applications concerning those verses.

Dear John,

Advanced

5 Find people who have "experienced" the content you are teaching. Invite them to class and interview them: How did they learn the content? How did they apply it? What were the results? Would they recommend the truth you're presenting? What advice would they give?

6 Develop a partnership with a fellow teacher to hold one another accountable for early lesson preparation. Agree together on the amount of time you feel is adequate for your preparation, and when you plan to schedule that time. Check on one another regularly.

AFFIRMATION

"Prepare Your Heart"

The person who teaches with style with a prepared heart has a **passion to communicate**—nothing can quench that desire! Passion is manifest in a **love for students**, and is borne out of a deep sense of **commission from God**. This teacher is doing the right thing by teaching—and knows it! He or she joyfully exercises the **high degree of preparation** needed to creatively teach the lesson. The necessary time is invested because this teacher is so utterly **convicted of the message's power**. There is power in content, but even more power in a life which demonstrates the truth. Therefore, the teacher with a prepared heart has **integrity with the message**. This teacher is humble enough to realize that without **dependence upon God**, no teaching will have its maximum impact.

The person whose heart is prepared is a person who Teaches with Style! By the grace of God, you can be that person!

Search me, O God, and know my heart; Try me, and know my anxieties; And see if there is any wicked way in me, And lead me in the way everlasting.

Psalm 139:23-24

I commit to Teach with Style through the continuing preparation of my heart—the nurturing of those internal beliefs which, when practiced, result in LifeChange in my students.

Signature/Date

EXTERNAL
BEHAVIORS

What causes teachers' feet to freeze to the floor, their hands to lock on the podium, their mouth to fill with cotton, and butterflies to swarm in their stomach? In this session you'll discover how to make your body your best teaching tool. So relax—and enjoy!

Translate what we know into doing what we know.

INSTRUCTION

Giant of INTIMIDATION

INTRODUCTION

Job if teachers is to apply scriptures.
Opposite of Faith = Fear.
Fear defeats more people than any other thing in the world.

BEHAVIORS 1

Note appendix R.2

Voice
- Adjust pitch,
- " pace

Focusing *your* **pupils helps your** *pupils* **focus.**

BEHAVIORS 2

Eyes

▼▼▼▼▼▼ BEHAVIORS 3

Face
Expressions should agree w/message you're leading/speaking.

•••••••• ▼ BEHAVIORS 4   Appendix 4

Gestures
Make them bigger if crowd is such. Adjust
Ex 32:19
Ezekiel 21:14 ┼

**Warning!
Hand outside
comfort zone!
Warning!**

BEHAVIORS 5   Communicates passion.

Posture
There are inappropriate postures.

Improve your use
of voice, eyes,
gestures, and
movement with
the innovative
diagnostic charts
in the Appendix
(pages A-1
through A-5).

BEHAVIORS 6

Appearance

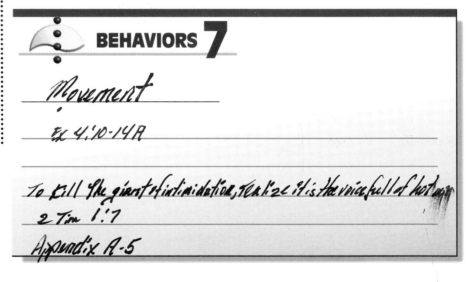

BEHAVIORS 7

Movement

Ex 4:10-14A

To kill the giant of intimidation, realize it is the voice full of hot air

2 Tim 1:7

Appendix A-5

Prof. Seemright's lecture on the harmony of the gospels was never taken seriously. He couldn't figure out why.

CONCLUSION

A Mastering the Minimum

The morning after attending Session Four, you're looking in the mirror preparing for the day. The main point of the message about the use of your body in teaching is still on your mind . . .

_____

_____

_____

B Looking for Boring Behaviors

Evaluate your teaching style below in light of the seven External Behaviors. (Record your score in the space.)

Never	Seldom	Sometimes	Usually	Always
1	2	3	4	5

1. My voice varies in pitch, volume, and intensity when I teach, either naturally or through deliberate effort. (_____)

2. I speak for extended periods of time in direct eye contact with my students, even when lecturing. (_____)

3. I am conscious of deliberately changing the expressions on my face a number of times during my class. (_____)

4. My hands and arms are comfortable pointers, illustrators, and attention-keepers when I teach. (_____)

5. I bend, sit, twist, stretch, and use any other body language available and appropriate when I teach. (_____)

6. Appearance is a consistent consideration when I plan my teaching sessions, and I vary it accordingly. (_____)

7. Over the course of a class session, I move in and out of all "four corners" of my classroom or teaching area. (_____)

Add up your total points and enter your score in the margin.

> **"** Session four's great, isn't it? I love to gesture and wave my hands when I teach—the students can't get their eyes off my hands! I love it when they give me 'high-fours!' Time for some great discussion now—and our quiz! **"**

My score: [＿＿＿]

30 – 35 Expert: making behaviors a priority!

25 – 29 Advanced: your students appreciate you!

20 – 24 Intermediate: could go either way!

15 – 19 Beginner: unclear on the concept!

10 – 14 Boring: what was the question?

C Building on Others' Behaviors

Think for a moment about teachers or communicators you have heard. Picture those for whom the external dimensions of teaching were a primary asset, and those who did not use their physical abilities to maximum potential.

From the teacher who used physical style well, I would love to learn how to . . .

_____

Watching the speaker who did not use physical style well makes me want to avoid . . .

_____

" For some of us, great physical delivery just comes naturally—know what I mean? Whatever our need, God is ready to help, right? So let's turn to His Word now to get some focused insight into physical delivery in Scripture. **"**

D Preparing to Change Some Behaviors

If your students thoroughly understood the seven External Behaviors, they would choose number _____ as being the behavior most evident in your life.

They would choose number _____ as the one needing the most improvement.

Try to recall a student conversation or incident which led you to answer as you did above:

_____

E Banishing Boredom from Behaviors

In the area you cited for improvement in D above, write down two steps you can take this week to make progress:

1. _____

2. _____

Voice: For More Than Just Speaking

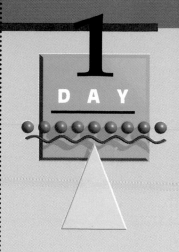

1

D A Y

Teacher Angelo is telling the group about the advice he received when his school's speech teacher observed one of his classes.

"The problem was that I couldn't keep the class's attention. They seemed interested at the start of the class, but after 15 or 20 minutes, they invariably drifted off.

"Well, the speech teacher had several really good ideas. But one was especially effective. He noticed that throughout the class, my voice matched my personality—intense, focused, and serious. While that approach got my students' attention, he said, it couldn't sustain it by itself. He suggested that I simply alter my vocal inflections and give my voice some variety.

"And you know, he was right. I've been making a conscious effort to vary my voice, and I can see a distinct difference in the students. It's one more thing to remember to do, but it's worth it!"

Truth / John 7:16, 21, 28, 33, 37 On one particularly dramatic occasion in the ministry of Christ, He used the tone and volume of His voice to accentuate His message. Note the progression of His responses to the crowds in the temple at Jerusalem in John 7:

> v. 16: "Jesus answered them . . ."
> v. 21: "Jesus answered and said to them . . ."
> v. 28: "Then Jesus cried out . . ."
> v. 33: "Then Jesus said to them . . ."
> v. 37: "Jesus stood and cried out . . ."

Read through this entire passage and note the changes in Jesus' voice, and how his speech reflects the identity and intent of those with whom He is interacting. Jesus was not intimidated by the sound of His own raised voice. He did more with His voice than just speak: He conveyed mood, expressed passion, and gained and held attention.

Transformation Are you comfortable with the broad range of pitches and volumes of your own voice—specifically, in the teaching environment? Why is it we will raise our voice in anger, whisper in serious tones, and speak in near-falsettos when we're exasperated—but never vary more than 5 percent from our natural, normal voice in the classroom?

If you're by yourself right now, experiment for a minute. (Or get alone later if now's not a good time.) Playing the part of Christ, read John 7 aloud according to His voice variations outlined above. Did you "cry out"? How about speaking "in a loud voice?" Did you answer gently, and also rebuke? Great! You're doing more with your voice than just speaking!

▶ **These seven devotionals will convince you that the Spirit of God wants to speak through your body!**

Warning: Don't let your voice be marketed as a cure for insomnia!

2

DAY

Eyes: Where Hearts Become Good Friends

 Teacher Steven Kirby is a businessman and a teacher. His experience with adults in the business world, as well as children and young people in church, lead him to make an interesting "confession."

"I've noticed that it's very difficult for me to make and keep eye contact when teaching a new group of adults—folks I don't know well. It seems much easier with children—and easier to keep their attention as a result. Why do you think that's the case?"

Richard replies: "You've touched on something we probably all struggle with. I think the issue is insecurity borne out of unfamiliarity. Remember that Jesus said we ought to become like little children—innocent, trusting, honest. Because children don't have hidden agendas, we can relax with them. With other adults, we're often not so sure what's behind the 'masks' we're looking at—and so we avoid looking! I think the goal is to take the initiative in establishing a climate of trust and honesty with adults in the classroom. The larger question is, 'How'?"

Truth / Matthew 6:22-23 The eyes are a gateway to the inner person, the real self. Read what Jesus had to say about the eye: **"The lamp of the body is the eye. If therefore your eye is good, your whole body will be full of light. But if your eye is bad, your whole body will be full of darkness."**

According to many scholars, this passage may have referred to a person's liberality with his or her possessions. Those who were greedy, refusing to share with others in need, had bad eyes. They couldn't sustain more than a fleeting glance. Their eyes constantly darted away. But those who had clear, upright consciences could look a person in the eye with no problem. Why? They were confident and secure in who they were; they felt no fear or intimidation.

Transformation Use eye contact as a method for increasing learning through establishing an atmosphere of trust and honesty.

First, ask yourself this question: As a teacher, do I avoid eye contact with my students—or with other adults? Don't feel bad if you do—most people you encounter tend to avoid direct eye contact. It may be nothing more than a bad habit—or it could be something more. Ask God to help you break the habit and to identify anything hindering your eyes from reflecting a pure heart.

Use your eyes to welcome your students and invite eye contact. The emotional warmth you exude will attract—and keep—*their* eyes.

Make sure the window of your soul has no smudges or smears.

> ▶ **To make oneself understood to people one must first speak to their eyes.**
>
> Napoleon

Face: Your Message for All the World to See

Teacher "Okay, teachers," Carla announces, "I have a little test for you. Unfortunately, I'm not exactly sure about the answer, but I'll make a suggestion and see what you think."

After the groans subside over the idea of a test, Carla poses her question: "What part of the body is the most important for enhancing teaching? Is it the eyes, for eye contact? The hands and arms for gesturing? The feet for moving around? The voice for speaking? I mean, they're all pretty critical when you think about it, right?"

Carla's silence while the group discusses causes them to press her for her ideas—"Okay, Carla, out with it. We can tell we haven't hit it yet!"

"You could all be right, but I think it's the face," she says, circling her own face with her finger. "Watch all the things I can say with my face." The group watches in amazement as Carla goes through a whole series of different expressions which speak silent volumes—all without a word.

"Wow!" Richard exclaims. "Let's 'face' it—you're right!"

Truth / Numbers 6:24-26 Throughout Scripture, "face" is a figure of speech for the whole person—whether human or divine. **"The LORD bless you and keep you; the LORD make His face shine upon you, and be gracious to you; the LORD lift up His countenance upon you, and give you peace."**

When God's face was shining upon Israel, His blessing was upon them. When He turned His face away, His favor was also withdrawn.

When a prophet fell on his face before God, he was bowing to show humility, not wanting to presumptuously enter God's presence. When sinners hid their faces from God, they were hiding their guilt.

Consistently in Scripture, the face is used as a metaphor for conveying the sentiments of the heart. It is the outward expression of inner conviction.

Transformation As a teacher, use your face to demonstrate the entire range of emotions which will support your teaching. If your subject is sad, let your face confirm it. If you want to generate enthusiasm, your face is where students will sense it first. Have you ever corrected an unruly student with arched eyebrows and a sideways glance? What teacher hasn't! You get the idea—take that which you do daily and purpose to use it more effectively in your teaching.

Try sitting in front of a mirror and doing a "Carla" (see above). When you see your own face and the catalog of communications it contains, you'll be encouraged to "face" the facts too. (Okay, you can lock the door!)

> **Exciting teaching is more of a choice than a talent.**

> ▶ If you say something amusing with a smile, nine times out of ten your listeners will smile right along with you.
>
> Milo Frank

4 DAY

Gesture: Giving Your Students a Hand

Teacher "Here's a pearl of wisdom I'd like to impart," Richard pronounces academically—but with a smile. "Since we're talking about using gestures to enhance teaching, I had a hunch about the word *jester*—you know, j-e-s-t-e-r—and our word *gesture* (Richard waves his arms in the air). What do you think I discovered in the unabridged dictionary?"

"I'm not sure," Angelo responds, "but I think we're about to find out."

"Both words are from the same root word. I knew it! Now don't miss this. What did a medieval jester do? He acted out what he was saying. His movements were an integrated part of his message. Jesters used gestures! Amazing, huh?"

"Uh, Richard," Carla asks, tentatively raising her hand, "did jesters later become known as fools because of their gestures? I'm a little worried."

"Hmm, let me get back to you on that, Carla!"

Truth / Acts 21:40 In some circumstances, gestures communicate as effectively as words—maybe even more so.

When the Apostle Paul was ready to preach, he spoke with the authority that comes from the power of the Holy Spirit. But that's not all. On one occasion, Paul was being accosted by an unruly mob. The Roman commander gave him permission to speak. But silencing the crowd was another matter. Paul spoke with the authority you would expect from an apostle—and he emphasized his words with a gesture.

> " 'I am a Jew from Tarsus, in Cilicia, a citizen of no mean city; and I implore you, permit me to speak to the people.' ... Paul stood on the stairs and motioned with his hand to the people."

Transformation Are you comfortable using your hands when you communicate? Or do you feel like a court jester when you try to use gestures? Here are some practical ideas to increase your comfort level with using gestures regularly:

First, draw a stick figure on a sheet of paper (that's you). Ask a friend to sit in one of your classes and keep a record of how many gestures and what kind you use. Assess where you need improvement.

Second, try standing in front of a mirror and extending your arms to the side, above your head, down low. Wrap your arms around yourself; hold a hand up high; wave in a way that would get your students attention. Sometimes it takes "breaking out of the box" to get started.

Practice gestures you don't presently do, and they will become a habit.

> **Remember: Jestering and gesturing only sound similar.**

▶ Just as the conductor of a symphony orchestra silently controls a complex organization, so the teacher can direct a class by a gesture, an inflection, or an expression.

Stanley Nelson

Posture: When Your Body Does the Talking

Teacher Liz is relating an experience that taught her the importance of body language in teaching with style.

"I attended a Bible study in a home where the atmosphere was purposely relaxed. A lot of young, previously unchurched people attended this study and the leader tried to maintain an atmosphere that would make everybody feel comfortable.

"Well, on this occasion the teaching was about spiritual warfare. We must be always on the alert, the leader was saying, because our enemy is always looking for ways to make us stumble.

"So far so good. But as he taught, he was settled back in an easy chair as though he were discussing that day's baseball scores. He didn't look like a person ready to engage in battle. I guess you could say his posture wasn't appropriate for the subject. And that really distracted me."

Truth / Revelation 1:12, 17 As with a person's eyes, voice, and face, a person's posture and bearing—his or her body language—is also a critical component of real communication.

The Apostle John was exiled on the Isle of Patmos when he was given a vision of Christ. John's entire being reacted to the risen glorified Lord, and John's posture pictured his heart's response.

> **"Then I turned to see the voice that spoke with me. And having turned I saw seven golden lampstands, and in the midst of the seven lampstands One like the Son of Man . . . And when I saw Him, I fell at His feet as dead."**

John's posture said, "You are the Lord. I am your servant. Tell me what you want me to do." And Jesus did. John's posture had said it all.

Transformation Think about your normal posture when you teach. Do you ever consciously change it to accomplish a specific purpose or to change the mood or tone of your teaching session?

• Standing straight behind a lectern communicates a serious intent—you want your class's attention. You mean business.

• Leaning on the wall or desk says, "Let's relax a moment."

• Sitting down—especially in a student desk—indicates a desire to relate to the students, to come down to their level.

• Pacing reveals energy and excitement.

• And staring silently out the window could say, "I need a moment to consider your actions," when behavior is disruptive.

Think of posture as one more tool in your Style Tool Kit—and use it!

> I have one tool to deliver my heart—my physical body. I must dedicate my body to serving my audience.
>
> Bruce H. Wilkinson

Have you ever stopped to listen to what your body is saying?

6 DAY

Appearance: Accent on the Message

Teacher "All right everybody," Carla says cheerfully, bursting into the room, "I've got some good news: Campbell's Department Store is having a fantastic sale! Since we've been talking about the relationship of our appearance to our teaching effectiveness, maybe this is a good time to fix up the old wardrobe, huh?"

"I knew Carla would eventually figure out a way to connect teaching and shopping," laughs Angelo.

As several people gather around the full-page ad Carla displays, Gayle feels a little frustrated. "Hey, wait a second. Is dressing like our students all that important? I'm teaching the junior-highers right now. Does that mean I have to try to look like one of them? I think it would be silly for a 38-year-old woman to try to look half her age!"

"True enough," Carla responds, "but dressing appropriately for your class doesn't mean imitating your students. It just means that you should be correct in what you wear. For instance, don't wear outdated fashions that draw attention. You don't have to be fadish—just contemporary within the bounds of good taste.

Truth / 1 Peter 3:3-4
"Do not let your beauty be that outward adorning of arranging the hair, of wearing gold, or of putting on fine apparel; but let it be the hidden person of the heart . . ."

In this verse, the word *adornment* translates the Greek word *kosmos*, which means an "ordered system."

So the Apostle Peter is saying that a woman's appearance should be an orderly one, consistent with her life's message, appropriate to the role of a godly woman in the church. This is an excellent principle for teachers—or anyone—to follow regarding appearance. If outward appearance distracts from the true life message—or teaching content—then it should be altered.

Transformation When an artist completes a beautiful landscape, or puts the last coat of varnish on a distinguished portrait, it is then time to pick the frame. The frame must serve and support the picture, giving definition and borders to a particular message. The artist selects a frame carefully, because it is the vehicle for presenting his work to the public.

When a teacher dresses for a particular class—whether planning for one day or a semester—appearance should be considered. Make sure your wardrobe and grooming provide the best possible frame for your message. Proper appearance eliminates a possible avenue of distraction.

> **Clothes don't make the man, but they can make the message better.**

> ▶ Your clothing and personal appearance speak for you before you've said a word.
>
> Milo Frank

Movement: Taking Style Where It's Never Been

Teacher Denise is smiling as the group gets into their discussion of "movement and style."

"All that moving around in class may work well with your students, Angelo. You teach high schoolers who are energetic themselves and who expect everybody to be that way—including their teachers. But most of my senior citizens would feel very uncomfortable—and I know I would—if I started trying to run all over the classroom. So how can I implement this aspect of teaching with style?"

"I think that's a good point, Denise," Gayle agrees. "I teach in a home Bible study setting. Usually we sit around the den in chairs or on the floor. Not much opportunity for movement at all."

Richard offers a comment that satisfies everyone: "It's not so much *how* you move—like how far or how fast—but *that* you move. If you have to teach seated, move to the edge of the chair occasionally. Movement of any sort is a change; and change draws attention; and not knowing what the next movement is means anticipation. That's what holds attention."

Truth / John 2:15 One of the most dramatic moments in Jesus' ministry came when He entered the temple in Jerusalem. Instead of a multitude of worshippers, Jesus found a crowd of moneychangers. How did Jesus react? He moved—quickly

> **"When He had made a whip of cords, He drove them all out of the temple, with the sheep and the oxen, and poured out the changers' money and overturned the tables."**

Jesus could have reacted by gathering a small crowd, standing in one place, and gently reasoning with the people about this unholy practice. But to teach the people the gravity of their sin, He moved. He ran around the temple porticos—no small area—overturning tables and driving out animals. The energy of his movement reinforced the passion of His message. No one was bored!

Transformation Think about the place you regularly teach: a classroom in a school, a Sunday school room in a church, a living room in a home, a conference room in an office. Now, let your thoughts run to the area immediately surrounding the place where you teach. Is there room for movement? There usually is lots of available room!

The simple variety of moving your class to a different place, or you moving to teach in a different part of the regular setting, can accentuate a particular point dramatically. Plan your points, then your path.

Movement is often a sign that there is indeed life in a person.

> **If your teaching has fewer movements than a symphony of the same length, you're in trouble!**

A Moment with Max

❝ I've been asked many times for advice on becoming more skilled in practicing the external behaviors of style. I'm only too glad to help! The way I got started—I haven't *always* taught with style, you know—was practicing a few "simple strokes" first, then venturing out into deeper water. In fact, I've written down some of the projects I tackled way back when I was just starting out. Now you can learn to use your body like 'ole Max here!

We're going to tackle 'gestures' first—our instructor's fourth point. So pick a project or two that will encourage you the most—and get your whole self into the act! ❞

Just Beginning

1 Read a familiar children's story out loud such as "Casey At the Bat" or "The Three Little Pigs" with exaggerated gestures. Better yet, read it to a group of children and lead them in doing the gestures and motions with you!

2 Practice gesturing in front of a mirror every night for a month. Exaggerate all of your gestures—just to get used to feeling your hands and arms moving in different ways. Work with all three dimensions spatially: height, breadth, and depth.

3 **Ask** a friend to observe your teaching and fill out a gesture grid like the one in the Appendix of this workbook. Have your friend mark every time you gesture. Mark the ranges vertically, horizontally, and in terms of depth. Repeat in six months to measure progress.

4 **Build** into your lesson plan places to use large gestures: how wide or tall something is; a shocking emotional description; pointing toward the horizon or heaven; hands on hips or knees in mock amazement. Making plans ahead of time increases your security.

Advanced

5 **Observe** a teacher who enjoys great freedom of movement with his or her arms and hands while speaking. Evaluate this speaker's gestures with a gesture grid (see #3 above). Compare your gestures with those of the teacher you observed. How can you improve?

6 **Video** tape your class so as to watch your gestures. Most teachers don't believe how little they gesture until they see themselves on video. Also video tape yourself practice-teaching at home. Review the tape and critique yourself, noting areas needing improvement.

AFFIRMATION

"Defeat the Giants"

The person who defeats the giants of Intimidation and Inhibition to teach with style has made a commitment to teach regardless of the cost. The teacher with style knows that the **voice** which never varies is the single greatest cause of boredom in the classroom. This teacher also knows that **eye** contact with students says more than many words—and that an expressive **face** communicates a whole range of powerful emotions. **Gestures**—the most intimidating use of the body— give teachers a second voice with which to teach. The teacher with style combines all of these with a **posture** suitable for the point, and an **appearance** suitable for the audience. Having prepared in this way, the teacher with style uses **movement** to carry the content to the student.

The person who defeats the giants is a person who Teaches with Style! By the grace of God, you can be that person!

For God has not given us a spirit of fear, but of power and of love and of a sound mind.

2 Timothy 1:7

I commit to Teach with Style through defeating the giants of Intimidation and Inhibition—the commitment to use my body to serve my students, which, when practiced, results in LifeChange in my students.

Signature/Date

PERSONALITY

Personality—every teacher has one! The critical issue is not "what kind?" but "what style?" Regardless of your personality type, using energy, variety, emotion, and other style intangibles can put your class in the palm of your . . . personality! So grab a smile and let's begin!

The giant of Inhibition

INSTRUCTION

INTRODUCTION

- *Gives dry mouth*
- *Fear leaving podium*

PERSONALITY 1

It is a choice, when one comes to a teaching situation.

- *Energy*
  - *Some have too much*

Mrs. Totally's
formula for success:
Energy =
Manifesting
Commitment to your
Class.

$E=mc^2$

PERSONALITY 2

Variety

Vary what we do.

1. *Planned*   2. *Unplanned*

PERSONALITY 3

"Drop your masks, students will drop theirs.
• Teach/Test principle

Transparency *to sin of self.*

Take principle from OT, take to NT say Christ disciples

1. _____
2. _____
3. _____
4. _____

Raise T.Q. = transparency quotient

PERSONALITY 4

Ecl. 3 = Time for everything

Humor

1. *Self*
2. *Be Alert (Look around)*
3. *Listen to Students*

"The Humor of Christ" by Elton (Trueblood?)

PERSONALITY 5

Neh 13:25

(overlaps w/Energy)
-Be

Emotion
Be emotional about your subject.

1 Thess 2:11

The downside of Miss Bright's creativity was finding hats that fit.

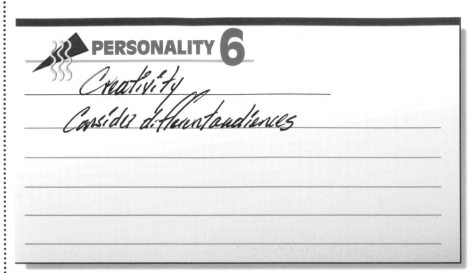

PERSONALITY 6

Creativity

Consider different audiences

PERSONALITY 7

Motivation

1. How to move them to do what you want done.
2. Focus upon needs of students.
   (Passionately committed to not boring God.)
3. Put self in lives of the hearer.
4. Maintain High Expectations
   • Expect things to happen.
   • Move away from Spirit of Inhibition

CONCLUSION

Self-motivation is not the prof's strong suit. It's not even in his wardrobe.

A Mastering the Minimum

People and their personalities can be a sensitive issue. What is the central truth you learned in this session which gives you freedom to maximize your personality in teaching?

_____

_____

_____

B Perspectives on Your Personality

Evaluate your teaching style below in light of the seven Personality traits in Session Five. (Record your score in the space.)

Never	Seldom	Sometimes	Usually	Always
1	2	3	4	5

1. I maintain a high energy level in my class to hold attention, either by choice or by natural teaching style. (_____)

2. I use variety in my personality (moods and expressions) to complement my content and teaching points. (_____)

3. My students and I have regular "below-the-surface" exchanges in class in which personal issues are shared. (_____)

4. Planned and confident use of humor—as part of my lesson plan—is a consistent aspect of my style. (_____)

5. Expressing emotional intensity to highlight or illustrate teaching points is within my "comfort zone." (_____)

6. My students would tell you that I am a "creative" teacher in terms of content presentation and application. (_____)

7. My personality reveals my high motivation to teach; in return, my students are motivated to learn. (_____)

Add up your total points and enter your score in the margin.

INTERACTION

"Did you ever feel you were a walking object lesson of the truth? That's how I feel about this session on personality! I love it! And you will too as we get deeper into it. Let's interact!"

My score: [   ]

30 – 35 Expert: making personality a priority!

25 – 29 Advanced: your students appreciate you!

20 – 24 Intermediate: could go either way!

15 – 19 Beginner: unclear on the concept!

10 – 14 Boring: what was the question?

C Personalities in Your Past

The seven traits identified in this session are those which make teaching more effective—because they help to hold attention and overcome boredom!

Think of a teacher in your past experience who exemplified one of the traits discussed in this session. Record here the person, the trait, and how that trait specifically impacted your learning experience—how that trait helped overcome boredom.

_____

_____

_____

" When you master this session, your students won't be able to find a 'needs improvement' area for Question D. All the traits will be shining through your personality—all the time! I've found that Teaching with Style not only has made me a better teacher—but a better person in every way. Can't you tell? **"**

D Your Personality and the Polls

If your students thoroughly understood the seven Personality traits, they would choose number _____ as being the trait most evident in your life.

They would choose number _____ as the one needing the most improvement.

Try to recall a student conversation or incident which led you to answer as you did above:

_____

E Personality and Practice

In the area you cited for improvement in D above, write down two steps you can take this week to make progress:

1. _____

2. _____

Energy: Fueling the Fire of Style

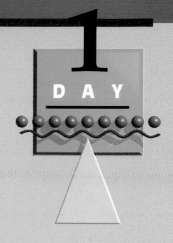

Teacher When it comes to a challenging task, Angelo's energy goes off the chart. But around people, he's not especially outgoing or dynamic. And until today, he thought he was destined to stay that way.

"I sat in on Mr. Brooks' class—we were doing peer reviews—and I was amazed," Angelo tells the group. "According to the personality test the faculty took, he and I have identical profiles. Both of us are driven to accomplish things in an exact, efficient way. We're methodical, quality-control oriented, and basically reserved around people.

"But he didn't allow that to dictate his style in the classroom. His energy level was off the chart! And he really entertains the kids as he's teaching them. And you should see the way they pay attention!"

"What was your conclusion, Angelo?" Gayle asks.

"That my lifestyle and my teaching style can be different!" Angelo replies. "That's a breakthrough for me. Now I've got to make it happen."

Truth / Acts 20:7b, 11 The Apostle Paul was like Angelo— consumed with tasks. Paul was driven with passion to preach the Gospel to all people everywhere, and to do so faithfully. But that doesn't mean Paul ignored people. To the contrary, he saw his task in terms of people, and brought his own off-the-chart energy level into his meetings. On one occasion, Paul stayed up all night to convey the content and urgency of his message to the new believers in Troas.

> "... Paul, ready to depart the next day, spoke to them and continued his message until midnight ... even till daybreak ...."

The result of this kind of energy? People were incredibly devoted to Paul—and his message of salvation in Christ.

Transformation Reality is, people have different energy levels. Some are naturally energetic, some are less so. Which are you?

Regardless of your natural inclination, here's the point: Teaching is normally not a place to "act naturally." Since teaching does require concentrated amounts of energy during a specific time, we must make a commitment to be "up" and produce the required energy level for that class.

We all have roles to fill in our lives, always striving for the ideal, rather than being satisfied with what comes naturally. Deciding to be energetic is simply deciding to fill the role of teacher to a higher degree. Rather than being superficial, as some might suggest, it is the highest form of sacrifice— giving up what is "normal" or "easy" for you for the sake of another.

The more power in the amplifier, the further the waves carry.

▶ **Learn from Scripture this week how your personality can fit perfectly in every teaching role you face!**

DAY 2

Variety: Never a Dull Moment!

Teacher "Let me tell you how I learned about the need for variety," says Carla, in mock embarrassment. "And from a group of elementary age children, no less."

"One morning I noticed a student moving her lips as I spoke during early morning administrative class time—you know, taking roll, signing absentee excuses, giving out lunch passes. She was saying to herself exactly what I was saying! I thought to myself, 'Is that child making fun of me?' Suddenly it hit me—she wasn't making fun, she was entertaining herself by saying all of my standard administrative lines along with me. She knew them by heart!

"I noticed her doing this off-and-on all day long! Was I so predictable that my students knew what I was going to say before I said it?

"The next day I purposefully didn't say a single thing that I normally say. Guess what the kids did? They watched me like a hawk. I had their attention all day—because of what I *didn't* say!"

Truth / Luke 20:24-25 Jesus was always unpredictable. He continually used variety and the element of surprise to keep His followers' interest.

When asked by a spy of the Pharisees whether or not it was right for the Jews to pay taxes to Caesar, Jesus' answer confounded His detractors to the point of silencing them:

> **" 'Show me a denarius. Whose image and inscription does it have?' . . . 'Caesar's.' . . . 'Render therefore to Caesar the things that are Caesar's, and to God the things that are God's.' "**

Because this was not the expected answer, it drew and held the attention of the crowd. It caused the crowd to stay close to Jesus so as to see and hear what other unforeseen things He might say or do. Variety lends the element of surprise to any setting.

Transformation Would your students, if asked, identify more with Carla's pupils or Jesus'? Hopefully the latter—and here's an exercise that may help:

Write out the normal sequence of events of your class—the order, proportion of time spent on each, and the number of total events. Now re-plan your next class by changing either the order, proportion, or number of events in your class time. Avoid routines which become too predictable. Students will begin coming to class expectantly, not knowing what is about to happen!

Remember: variety = surprise = getting and holding attention.

> ▶ Even pudding needs a theme.
>
> Winston Churchill

When students answer questions before you ask, it's time for variety.

Transparency: Style from the Inside Out

Teacher "One of the concerns I've had about the Sunday school class I lead is building intimacy," Denise confides. "Folks my age usually don't reveal too much about their feelings, and I didn't really know what to do.

"Then I read an article about how groups tend over time to reflect the traits of their leaders. It made me wonder whether the lack of intimacy in the class was a reflection of the leader—me! And I think it was. I felt like good teaching was sticking right to the lesson without too much diversion.

"Well, when I followed the advice in the article, and began building in more of my personal feelings and experiences as illustrations of the Scriptural truths, my class began to respond. I think they needed to know I could handle their transparency—and the only way I could prove it to them was to be transparent myself!"

Truth / 2 Corinthians 6:11-13 The Apostle Paul was certainly concerned with excellence. But that doesn't mean he was emotionally stiff. Rather, he was a man of deep passion for his ministry, as well as deep commitment to those who responded to him.

"O Corinthians! We have spoken openly to you, our heart is wide open. You are not restricted by us, but you are restricted by your own affections. Now in return for the same . . . you also be open."

In 2 Corinthians, Paul reveals more of his heart—is more unashamedly transparent—than in any other New Testament book. It is primarily from this book that we, as his "students," are able to relate his theology to his personal life—and conclude that it works! Even the great apostle knew that his charges needed to see what was on the inside of him.

Transformation How often does your class see who you are as a person? How willing are you to divulge the "real you"?

If you begin to relate to your class anecdotes from your personal or family life—for example, a fear, a victory, a defeat, a challenge, a difficult incident, an embarrassing experience, a moment of pride, or a concern— you will be amazed at the new level of attentiveness and involvement. People are interested in people! As you open up and begin to share yourself with your class, you will discover that your students will respond in kind. Try using small rotating groups of four students each to meet occasionally to share different facets of their life story and experiences with each other.

Open up! Your students will respect your transparency . . . and copy it.

Transparency is infectious—be a carrier.

> "Seeing right through" a person is not the same as transparency!

4 DAY

Humor: Earning the Right to Be Serious

Teacher Liz Darby tends to be all business, both at work and in her Bible study. But this week she learned the importance of lightening up the atmosphere of her class with humor.

"A guest speaker came to the Bible study to share about her inner-city ministry and to ask for financial support," Liz says. "You would think that she would spend the whole time very seriously, showing us what the Bible says about our responsibility to the poor, telling us about her successes in her work, and making an appeal for gifts.

"Not this woman—at least not right away. She had the group rolling with laughter for the first half of her talk. She told stories of her experiences in ministry, and interacted with our group like a talk-show host.

"And then, perfectly timed, just when things were quieting down, she got serious. After we were relaxed by the laughter, she hit us with the hard truth. And we responded."

Truth / Matthew 23:24 Jesus was a man on a mission—a deadly serious one. But that doesn't mean He never used humor. Even as He soundly condemned the religious leaders of the Jewish nation for their hypocrisy, Jesus used a metaphor that is quite funny when you stop to picture its meaning:

> "'Blind guides, who strain out a gnat and swallow a camel!'"

While we don't often laugh while reading the Bible, it is nevertheless filled with ancient Near Eastern forms of wit and humor. When the situation called for it, Jesus ridiculed His opponents with biting humor. The absurdity of an elite Pharisee straining at a gnat while swallowing a camel undoubtedly made many of Jesus' listeners laugh—at the Pharisees' expense! There were probably many in the crowds who were first attracted to His spiritual truth through His humor.

Transformation The first responses of teachers when encouraged to use humor in class is "I'm just not funny," or "I couldn't tell a good joke if my life depended on it." Fortunately, you do not *personally* need to be funny (that's different than using humor), and even better, your life doesn't depend on it.

If you are familiar with *Reader's Digest* magazine, you're half-way home. Bringing one joke to class each week and telling it (preferably the cornier the better), will earn you a good laugh (either for the joke or your effort!)

Don't forget to tell a joke on yourself occasionally—it builds character!

The class that laughs together learns together!

> Humor breaks down barriers that all the passion, determination, and fiery oratory sometimes can't demolish.
>
> James W. Robinson

Emotion: Welcoming Feelings to Your Class

Teacher "One of my students was telling the class about the recent death of a beloved grandparent," Gayle says to the group. "Suddenly, she burst into tears, even sobs.

"You should have seen the class change. Other kids gathered around her, and some of the students even cried with her. I started crying, too. It was a special moment for our class. All the walls were down, the differences forgotten. We shared a moment of real sympathy and understanding. It was an emotional moment, and it made me realize that we don't have many such times in the classroom.

"As I thought about the powerful reaction of the class, I wondered if it would be acceptable to initiate emotion when teaching through a lesson. I don't mean to manipulate people but simply use emotions to initiate a response. Is this a legitimate element of style?"

Truth / 2 Samuel 6:12, 14 Some people wrongly believe that Christians and Stoics have something in common. They think that true Christian maturity means not reacting emotionally in any situation, but accepting all things "stoically" as manifestations of the divine will. Nothing could be further from the truth.

In the Bible, emotions aren't squelched; they are freely expressed within the boundaries of self-control and consideration for others. When the ark of the covenant was restored to its proper place in Jerusalem, David knew that such a great event demanded a whole-souled emotional response. So he led the Israelites in full, uninhibited rejoicing.

> **"So David went and brought up the ark of God from the house of Obed-Edom to the City of David with gladness. . . . Then David danced before the LORD with all his might."**

Transformation In almost all your teaching situations, you can encourage your students to express feelings of joy, excitement, enthusiasm—even grief, conviction, legitimate guilt, and rejoicing.

Remember, however, that Western cultures do not encourage the outward manifestation of emotion, especially by leaders and by males. (This is totally opposite to the ancient Biblical cultures where emotional expression was normal and commonplace.) Most people choose not to express their emotions; it is usually an involuntary response.

So be sensitive, and be a learner yourself. How are you expressing your own emotions? Ask for God's freedom and balance to do so. Gradually you will see a new level of intimacy develop between you and your students.

Teaching is definitely something worth getting emotional over.

> No tears in the writer, no tears in the reader.
>
> Robert Frost

Creativity: Unleashing the Style Within

Creativity: Unleashing the Style Within

 Teacher "I've got to tell you," Steven Kirby confesses, "it's hard to be creative, to come up with new ways to teach every week.

"The business folks meeting for Bible study in my small conference room over lunch are busy and have a million things on their minds—what happened that morning and what's coming that afternoon. I mean, I can barely cover a verse or two and apply it to their lives. I don't know how in the world I'm supposed to do all kinds of creative stuff as well."

"But wait, Steven," Carla responds. "I think you're confusing creativity with methodology. Using overheads, doing projects, and role playing are all methods. We're not talking about that. We're talking about inventiveness, ingenuity, and originality—traits God has given to every person. There's a world of creativity in each of us waiting to be set free. You can be totally creative with nothing but a Bible. Remember, Jesus had none of our modern teaching tools, but was continuously creative in applying truth."

Truth / Colossians 1:16 When we are creative, we imitate Him who created everything we see.

"For by Him all things were created that are in heaven and that are on earth, visible and invisible, whether thrones or dominions or principalities or powers. All things were created through Him and for Him."

Stop for a moment and consider the creativity of God. Think about the variety of designs, colors, shapes, and sizes of God's creation. Think about the animal and plant kingdoms, the human body, the complexity of a single plant cell, the molecular structures in the world. It's the fitting together of complex and varied parts into unified wholes that takes our breath away.

If that were not enough, God has created mankind in His image, a reflection of His character and His ways. When we look at human accomplishments in the arts and sciences, it is obvious that creativity is one of the defining characteristics of those made in the image of God.

Transformation *Creative* is not synonymous with *artistic*. You don't have to be an artist to be creative; you only have to be alive. Creativity in some form is an inherent part of our makeup.

If you have ever thought that you're not very creative, take this moment to acknowledge your error. If you deny your own creativity, you suggest a deficiency in God's creativity, for *you* are made in *His* image. Pray this prayer right now: *Lord, please help me to understand—and release—Your creativity in me. May all my teaching reflect Your creative ways!*

> ▶ Creativity is not so much the "what" as the "how." The ways in which different musicians play the same set of notes may be totally a matter of their creativity.

People are creative. Teachers are people. Teachers are creative.

Motivation: Style and the Big Picture

Teacher Richard Douglas has been listening intently as the class has discussed the importance of personality and style.

"So far," Richard says, "we've been talking about things that have to do with in-class presentation and response. And those are important things to talk about. But we mustn't forget what, I believe, is our ultimate concern: lifechange. We want to motivate people to take what we teach them and *apply it to their lives*. Motivation for lifechange is our biggest challenge."

"Good point, Richard," Angelo says. "And motivation has to be tied to something beyond the present. If my students don't see how the content of my class is tied to a bigger goal, they aren't motivated. There's no way my kids would be motivated to do the work required for an advanced placement test if they couldn't imagine themselves as successful professionals someday in the future. If they didn't have that goal in mind, they would take a 'so-what' attitude toward the work I ask them to do."

Truth / Hebrews 11:24-26 Richard and Angelo are right on target. The author of Hebrews makes a clear connection between present activity and future reward.

> ". . . Moses . . . (chose) to suffer affliction with the people of God . . . esteeming the reproach of Christ greater riches than the treasures in Egypt; for he looked to the reward."

The Biblical way is to take the long view, to see the big picture, to imagine how today's small step can connect with a larger realm of success. Had Moses not been confident of a higher purpose, a greater end, what motivation would he have had for the risks he took? He was willing to sacrifice everything for the goal of redeeming Israel from bondage. And his willingness was a self-generated and self-sustained decision—the evidence of true and lasting motivation—derived from the initial promise of God.

Transformation Use the ABCs of motivation every time you teach a point of content, regardless of the class: **A B**enefit or **C**onsequence. In every area of life, benefits or consequences accrue as we act. For every point you make in your lesson, find the Bs of learning and apply them. Also point out the Cs of not learning, and encourage your students to avoid them. Benefits and consequences are excellent sources of long-term motivation—once they are understood and internalized.

To be motivational, the Bs and Cs must be tangible, relevant, achievable, measurable, and appropriate to the age or maturity of your students. Nothing quenches motivation like expectations set too high.

> Motivation in life has much to do with motives in life. It's the same in teaching.

It takes a motivated teacher to produce motivated students.

APPLICATION

A Moment with Max

" Boy, do I have some exciting projects for you this time—they're guaranteed winners! I've astounded thousands of students—well, 100 or more, at least—with these very projects! They work for me, and will for you, too. We're focusing on trait number two from this session—**Variety.** As your instructor explained, VARIETY keeps attention focused. And where attention is focused, boredom is nowhere to be found. So whether you're ▶ **just beginning,**

● **ready for a challenge,**

■ **or an advanced teacher,**

you can pick a project and banish boredom— this week! "

Just Beginning

1 Reverse the order of the events in your teaching time. Whatever normal routine you follow, do the opposite. The point here is not confusion, but attention focused by variety. When students don't know what's "next," they pay closer attention.

2 Alter the proportion of time spent on activities in class. Give the largest proportion of time to whatever activity normally gets the least amount. For instance, calling roll: do mini-autobiographies as you call each name, helping students get to know each other better.

3 Arrange for a guest lecturer or substitute teacher to take your class for a day or period. But don't leave! Stay and participate, adding variety through having a different speaker whom your students are not used to (make sure your guest teaches with style!).

4 Rearrange your class room regularly—but not predictably! It is even more attention-holding to arrange your class on the basis of variety in teaching: work groups, discussion groups, lecture, debate, or other method.

Advanced

5 Cast a group of friends as "actors" who will teach the bulk of your content through dramas, role plays, dramatic monologues, skits, or other dramatic methods. "Stage" a dramatic event which your students don't know is fabricated to make a teaching point; then explain.

6 Take your students to a different location for the class session. Arrange transportation and adhere to schedules so as not to cause inconvenience. Make it a surprise until you get there. Have the students evaluate the impact of the change in setting.

For You have formed my inward parts; You have covered me in my mother's womb. I will praise You, for I am fearfully and wonderfully made; Marvelous are Your works, And that my soul knows very well.

Psalm 139:13-14

"Teach Unnaturally"

The person who teaches with style moves beyond the limits of his or her natural style of teaching. An **energy** level is present which is contagious. Students respond and are kept on the edge of attentiveness by the **variety** used—always a new look, a new plan, a new adventure in learning. Teachers with style promote openness and sharing by employing **transparency**—and then balancing serious moments with healthy doses of **humor. Emotions**, and their liberal and timely expression, are a prerequisite for teaching with style. Undergirding all other personality skills is **creativity:** mixing just the right blend of personality and style. The end result? **Motivation**, that priceless treasure that moves students beyond today into tomorrow.

The person who doesn't act naturally is a person who Teaches with Style! By the grace of God, you can be that person!

I commit to Teach with Style through moving beyond my natural style—to use my personality in genuine and creative ways, which, when implemented, result in LifeChange in my students.

Signature/Date *2·16·02*

METHODOLOGY

To know what makes great methodology, you have to ask a Great Teacher—like Jesus Christ. In this session you'll discover some startling facts about the methods Christ used, and why. And best of all, you'll learn how you can teach like Him—using His methods!

INTRODUCTION

Methods of Jesus

_____

_____

_____

_____

_____

METHODOLOGY 1

used for certain things.

Lecture
* Math 5:12*
• Good for large groups + delivery of content.

_____

_____

_____

_____

Mrs. Linyap considers it her moral duty to perpetuate the tradition that all lectures must be boring.

METHODOLOGY 2

Christ used 35-50 Parables.

Stories + Illustrations...

_____

1. _____   3. _____

2. _____   4. _____

_____

_____

METHODOLOGY 3

Visual Aids

○ Deu 6:6-9

METHODOLOGY 4

Questions & Answers

Once when I was
yust a wittle kid . . .

METHODOLOGY 5

Discussion

Directed

Guided

Random

METHODOLOGY 6

Drama

Mo gradually realizes that the Question and Answer method works best with

more than one person present.

METHODOLOGY 7

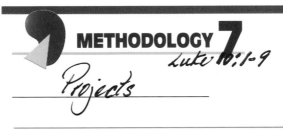

Luke 10:1-9

Projects

CONCLUSION

A Mastering the Minimum

You're discussing methodology with a teacher who didn't attend Teaching with Style. Your friend doesn't believe methods make that much difference. What is your one-sentence response?

_____

_____

_____

B Measuring <u>Your</u> Methodology

Evaluate your teaching style below in light of the seven Methodologies. (Record your score in the space.)

Never	Seldom	Sometimes	Usually	Always
1	2	3	4	5

1. When I lecture, it is by choice, not from lack of planning; I use lecture because it accomplishes a specific goal.   (_____)

2. The majority of the stories I tell as illustrations are of my own creation.   (_____)

3. In every class I teach, I introduce a visual aid of some kind, even if it is just painting a detailed word picture.   (_____)

4. When students ask questions, I answer with a question to lead them in self-discovery of the truth.   (_____)

5. The discussions which take place in my class are as a result of planning as well as spontaneous ones.   (_____)

6. Drama, role play, dramatic readings, skits, and scripted plays are part of my teaching methodology.   (_____)

7. I assign out-of-class projects to my students to reinforce what I have been teaching in class.   (_____)

Add up your total points and enter your score in the margin.

"I don't know about you, but I feel GREAT about what we've accomplished in this course! Let's squeeze every ounce of lifechange out of this last session. And by the way—this is our last quiz!"

My score: [ ]

30 – 35 Expert: making methods a priority!

25 – 29 Advanced: your students appreciate you!

20 – 24 Intermediate: could go either way!

15 – 19 Beginner: unclear on the concept!

10 – 14 Boring: what was the question?

◆C Masters of Methods

Some teachers seem to excel at one or two particular teaching methods—perhaps stories, maybe drama. Think about two teachers you have seen who were masters of their methodology—they had made a fine art out of a method.

One teacher used ___*application*___ more effectively than any teacher I've ever seen by . . .

_____

Another teacher was a master at _____ . He or she would astound us by . . .

_____

◆D Your Most-Noticed Methods

If your students thoroughly understood the seven Methodologies, they would choose number _____ as being the one most evident in your life.

They would choose number _____ as the method most needing improvement.

Try to recall a student conversation or incident which led you to answer as you did above:

_____

◆E Moving Toward More Methodology

In the area you cited for improvement in D above, write down two steps you can take this week to make progress:

1. _____

2. _____

"Like the notes say, we're moving toward more methods in our teaching. And you know what else? We're moving toward a greater appreciation of God's style as seen in Scripture, aren't we? His methods were awesome! Let's begin our final week of devotions and see what our group of teachers is learning this week.**"**

Lecture: Telling the Truth

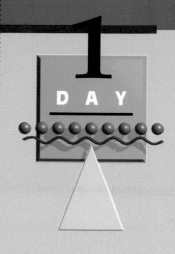

Teacher "After a recent church service in which I delivered the sermon," Richard says, "a visitor told me how much she enjoyed my 'lecture.' I was stunned. Even a little offended. I never thought of a sermon as a lecture, especially one I felt so deeply about. But as I thought about her remark, I became more comfortable with it. A sermon *is* a lecture in many ways."

"Richard, why do you think you felt negatively about your sermon being called a lecture?" Carla asks.

"Academic conditioning, I guess. Aren't we taught by example in most educational environments that lectures are dry and boring? I must admit that I gave some thought to why the person applied the term 'lecture' to my speaking. Maybe I was dry and boring!" Richard replies.

"But 'dry and boring' is a function of style, not method," Gayle says. "Since Jesus lectured so much, lecturing must be a good method to use. The key is to keep it from being boring—which is what style is all about."

Truth / Matthew 5:1-2 In Jesus' most famous sermon, the Sermon on the Mount, the Master Teacher gave a clear example of a lecture—one person verbalizing information to others.

"And seeing the multitudes, [Jesus] went up on a mountain, and when He was seated His disciples came to Him. Then He opened His mouth and taught them . . . ."

If you check your Bible, you'll see that this sermon, the most famous lecture in history, runs for several pages. But you can bet that not a single person sitting through it was bored! And note that lectures can be interrupted for the occasional question, or highlighted by another method at appropriate places. The point here is that Christ's teaching dominated the event—one person speaking the truth to multitudes.

Transformation If you look up the word *lecture* in a thesaurus, you'll find that the synonyms don't convey boredom. They simply mean "to communicate." A lecture in itself is neither boring nor exciting; the way it's delivered makes the difference.

Most teachers feel they should avoid lectures because of the potential for boring students—conditioning, remember? Teachers need a change of mind regarding lectures! After that, interesting lectures are next.

Plan to deliver a lecture soon. Remember, that means that you will do most of the talking. So plan plenty of attention-getters, as well as a lot of variety to hold your audience's interest.

Sometimes students need nothing more than a good lecture!

> ▶ **Discover evidence this week that all the great teaching methods of history can be found in Scripture!**

Stories: Finding Truth in Life

Teacher Denise Farris usually has wise words for the group. Today is no exception.

"Since we're discussing methods that work well for us, I want to mention stories," Denise says. "Stories are easy to listen to and fun to think about. What's more, they sink an idea deep into your heart. Sometimes you think you understand a principle from the Scriptures, but when you hear a good story illustrating it, you understand it better. Stories help you reflect—and the senior citizens that I teach are in a reflective time of life.

"I try to tell a lot of stories, especially from 20th-century American history, because they know a lot about that and can identify with the stories. Also, seniors grew up in an era when story-telling was more commonplace. Today's children and middle adults are much more visually oriented."

Truth / Matthew 13:1-3 Nobody knew how to tell a story like Jesus. We recall them as parables—stories Jesus made up to illustrate a truth.

On one occasion, when large crowds of people were gathered to hear Him, He wanted to convey the truths of the kingdom of God. But instead of straight lecture, Jesus used stories to make His points.

> **"Jesus went out of the house and sat by the sea. And great multitudes were gathered together to Him . . . . Then He spoke many things to them in parables . . . ."**

Parables were the story form Jesus used most often. *Parable* is from two Greek words, *para* and *bole*, which together mean "to throw alongside." A parable was a story "thrown alongside" a truth to illustrate it. Parables served at least two primary purposes in Jesus' teaching ministry: First, a story provided a frame of reference for the truth presented. Second, a story caused thought, separating those who were hungry for truth from those who weren't.

Transformation One four-letter word is all that is needed to convey the essence of storytelling: *like*. Turn to Matthew 13 and see how often Jesus says, "The kingdom of heaven is *like* . . . ." A story takes a truth, an abstract idea, and makes it concrete, or real, in the heart and experience of the listener. By recounting a picture from real life, a story says, "See, here's what this idea is like."

You use this word in daily conversation often. You cast one thing alongside another to make something clearer. Purpose to tell a story the next time you teach. When you do, you will be teaching like Jesus.

> Information's pretty thin stuff unless mixed with experience.
>
> Clarence Day

A story carries a truth from the library to life and back again.

Visual Aid: Picturing the Truth

Teacher Some in the group are questioning the use of so many visual aids in teaching. They feel that doing so deemphasizes reading skills. But Carla presents a different point of view.

"I have found that with my elementary students, visuals work perfectly. Perhaps it's because they grew up watching so many hours of television and movies—especially the older elementary students. And yes, it's a shame that kids today are less auditory and more visual. But what can we do? Visual communication is what they've come to expect. Is it wrong to use a teaching method that communicates in a way that kids are used to?"

Gayle Henson agrees with Carla: "I think you're right, Carla. After all, Jesus did the same thing. He used a lot of illustrations based on agriculture because He lived in a primarily agrarian society. He knew that's what people would relate to. And so He knew that's how He could communicate His point."

Truth / John 15:1-2, 5 Jesus didn't limit His teaching methods to either visual or auditory. On His final night with His disciples before His crucifixion, He passed through vineyards after leaving the upper room to go to the Mount of Olives. Stopping to use the elements of the vineyard—vines, branches, and fruit—as a visual aid, Jesus showed the disciples that they had to remain in Him if they were to bear spiritual fruit.

> **"I am the true vine, and My Father is the vinedresser. Every branch in Me that does not bear fruit He takes away; and every branch that bears fruit He prunes, that it may bear more fruit. . . . I am the vine, you are the branches. He who abides in Me, and I in him, bears much fruit; for without Me you can do nothing."**

Transformation Just as a story is a verbal comparison or illustration of a truth, so a visual object or presentation is a physical comparison or illustration. When you show students something visually, you are saying, "It's like this object you can see . . . ."

What physical or other visual illustrations or comparisons can you take to your next class? They are easy to discover. First, determine the point you are making. Next, ask yourself what the point is like in your own experience. Then find an object or other visual means to represent that point. Visual aids can come from any source. You can create an acetate visual for an overhead projector, or use a physical object. If you can see it, use it!

Not only will your students see your point, they'll remember it too!

> ▶ **Things seen are mightier than things heard.**
>
> **Alfred, Lord Tennyson**

Visual aids can help your students "see" your point more clearly.

Questions & Answers: Clarifying the Truth

Teacher Liz Darby is sharing with the group about the power of using question-and-answer sessions in the Bible study she leads. "With my singles Bible study, I use the question and answer method all the time. It's teaching through challenge. I use questions to make them think—to make them defend what they believe. That's why I'm not at all afraid to play 'devil's advocate.' These people hear so much that's not true in our culture. And many of them don't have solid Bible backgrounds yet. I consider questions and answers one of the best methods for clarifying beliefs through interactive questioning."

This strikes a chord with Richard: "Looking back, I think some of the most effective learning in my seminary classes was done using the Socratic method. The prof would call on us, we would rise to our feet, and he would question us on our understanding of theology. It was brutal, but effective!"

Truth / Matthew 21:23-25a Jesus used questions constantly, especially in interacting with those who opposed Him. On one occasion, a question intended to trap Him was answered with a question:

> "... the chief priests and the elders of the people confronted Him as He was teaching .... But Jesus answered and said to them, 'I also will ask you one thing, which if you tell Me, I likewise will tell you by what authority I do these things: The baptism of John, where was it from? From heaven or from men?' "

In this situation, as in so many others when He used questions, Jesus' questions made people think. Instead of spoon feeding people by giving them the immediate answer, He often asked the right questions to help them come up with the answer themselves. In this way, He demonstrated the "self-discovery" benefit of questions and answers as a teaching method.

Transformation Often questions arise out of the moment. An important part of teaching with style is developing a "feel" for asking the right questions spontaneously, meeting the needs of the moment.

Here is the simplest, yet most profound, rule for creating great interaction in class through questions: Never—NEVER, EVER—ask a question which a student can answer with a Yes or a No. Use the five Ws and the H (Who, What, Why, When, Where, and How) to transform simple questions into thought provokers requiring longer answers.

And don't be alarmed if you hear a strange buzzing sound. It's only the wheels of your students minds' turning!

Facts become useful when they're the answer to a question.

> "I'm glad you asked me that question. I didn't realize that the answer was in me until you asked!"

Discussion: Learning the Truth Together

Teacher "We've talked about a lot of great teaching methods in these sessions," Angelo says. "We've all learned from the give-and-take—which demonstrates the value of another method: discussion. We've been our own object lesson!

"Frankly, that doesn't surprise me," he continues. "I've discovered that discussions—even structured debates—have been one of the best teaching methods for my high school students.

"If I moderate, insist on courtesy and fairness, help clarify meanings, and act as a referee when things get a little too lively, then discussions and debates are truly exciting—especially when the kids have done research prior to class and therefore are well prepared."

Truth / Luke 24:15, 17, 27 Jesus taught by discussion. After He had risen from the dead, two of His followers were discussing the astonishing events surrounding His crucifixion. Jesus joined them on the road to Emmaus, hiding His identity at first:

> "... while they conversed and reasoned ... Jesus Himself drew near and went with them .... And He said to them, 'What kind of conversation is this that you have with one another as you walk and are sad?' ... And beginning at Moses and all the Prophets, He expounded to them in all the Scriptures the things concerning Himself."

In this setting, two discussions took place: First, the disciples on the road discussed events they didn't understand; namely, the crucifixion of Christ. Second, when Christ joined them, He inquired about their discussion and joined in. Instead of starting a lecture, He ate supper with them and continued the talk, clarifying what they didn't understand.

Transformation Often when we talk about ideas and issues with others, our own thoughts begin to jell, becoming beliefs, even convictions. At best, discussions promote inquiry, learning, and tolerance for opposing views. At worst, they can quickly deteriorate into arguments.

Assign a topic and prepare to discuss different points of view. Allow dissent, disagreement, and dialogue—but not insults, emotional outcries, or personal attacks.

It's important to clarify at the end. What was learned? What was accomplished? The issue doesn't have to be completely settled, but there should be enough closure to move ahead to the next class with no loose ends.

> I love to attend discussions to discover what I think about the subject at hand!

Discussion causes nuggets to surface in the mind.

Drama: Acting Out the Truth

 Teacher "OK, guys," says Gayle, "what teaching method do you think I use most with my junior-highers?"

"That's easy," Angelo quips. "Sedatives!"

After the laughter, Gayle continues: "No, not quite! Actually, I've found a method that taps into their strongest desire—to perform and be noticed—while adding support to their strongest insecurity, which is insecurity about who they are.

"The secret? Drama! By using all sorts of dramas—spontaneous, role plays, scripted—the kids really get into the lesson. The outgoing ones will act on the spot. And the less comfortable ones will also do great when given a script to rely on.

"Acting out the truth gives these kids a whole new perspective—it's as if drama places them *in* the truth instead of outside it looking on. I think it's the most neglected method we have."

Truth / Matthew 21:1-3 At key moments in His ministry, Jesus used dramatic means to teach important truths. One such moment was His triumphal entry into Jerusalem.

". . . Jesus sent two disciples, saying to them, 'Go into the village opposite you, and immediately you will find a donkey tied, and a colt with her. Loose them and bring them to Me. And if anyone says anything to you, you shall say, "The Lord has need of them," and immediately he will send them.' "

When it was time for Christ to enter Jerusalem in preparation for His crucifixion, He chose a very dramatic way that highlighted Old Testament prophecies concerning the Messiah. It drew attention to His entry, got many people involved, and caused people to think about His identity.

Transformation Using dramas in class can be problematic—particularly at both ends of the age scale. Both young children and senior saints may find this method a little difficult to implement. But with careful planning even they can participate in simple role plays.

The greatest misconception about the use of drama is that it must be scripted, with costumes, three acts, and a curtain call! Wrong! Instead, watch for an issue which surfaces in your own experience this week. If it raises an issue worth considering, craft a simple way for several students to use it as a spontaneous drama. Sometimes non-scripted role plays and dramas produce the most surprising learning experiences—so be ready!

Warning: Jr. Highers may think "role play" means a food fight.

> ► **When you hear information, you retain 20%. When you hear it and see it, you retain 50%. If you hear it, see it, and do it, retention goes to 90%.**
>
> **Bob Boylan**

Projects: Putting the Truth to Work

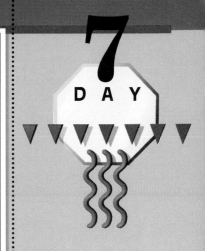

Teacher "My Bible study group presents a unique challenge," Steven Kirby relates. "The members rarely see each other during the week. We work in our different businesses, go to different churches, and have different social networks, so there's little interaction outside of our once-a-week meeting. The challenge is to keep them involved in the content of our weekly lesson even though they have no accountability with other group members outside of class.

"I got the answer from Jesus—good source, huh? I've started giving them a project to work on based on our weekly lesson. Remember how Jesus sent the disciples out to preach after they'd been with Him? Same model. I teach, we talk, they go and do, they return and report—then we do it again. It's been going great, with one problem. They want to talk and ask so many questions about the projects that it's hard to get to the new content!"

"I could live with a problem like that!" sighs Angelo.

Truth / Luke 9:1-2, 6 Jesus was a Jewish teacher and followed the pattern of the rabbis in Israel. Wherever a rabbi went, his students went. What the rabbi did, the students learned to do. Therefore, at the right time, Jesus sent His own students out to put into practice the very things He had been teaching them by word and by deed:

> **"Then He called His twelve disciples together and gave them power and authority over all demons, and to cure diseases. He sent them to preach the kingdom of God and to heal the sick. . . . So they departed and went through the towns, preaching the gospel and healing everywhere."**

And it was not just the project that was important. Verse 10 describes how when they returned, Jesus talked about what they learned.

Transformation There are excellent reasons for assigning projects to students: accountability for application of content, learning to work in teams, self-discovery, opportunities not available in the classroom, and the chance to appreciate success—and failure!

In addition, you will see varying levels of creativity, self-discipline, self-motivation, insecurity, and a healthy degree of tension over "fear of the unknown" surface in your students.

Projects, in terms of lifechange, may be the most effective tool at a teacher's disposal. In terms of use, they may be the most underused.

Your project: get your students involved in a project this week!

> ▶ A project is simply "projecting" truth from one situation—the classroom—to another—LIFE!

Truth untested may be truth unlearned.

A Moment with Max

" Wow! We have tackled some great projects in this course! Think back for a minute: we did Universal Principles, Biblical Characteristics, Internal Beliefs, External Behaviors, and Personality. But you know, the bottom line is doing it—doing some method, right? I mean, when you get all that other stuff down, you still walk into class and everybody's looking at you— waiting. Don't you just love the pressure—the challenge!? It's great! And to make sure you're ready, here are some projects on point number three in this session, Visual Aids. So let's go out with a BANG, and make these projects the best yet. And God bless you and your students as you keep on Teaching with Style! "

Max!

Just Beginning

1 Take your class to see what you are teaching about. If it's government, go to the courthouse or capital. If it's disease, go to the hospital. If it's history, go to a museum. <u>Show</u> them in person the thing or concept you are talking about in class.

2 Assign your students the responsibility for creating visual aids to illustrate and support an upcoming class topic. Make sure they have materials and skills to accomplish the task. Save the visual aids over the length of the class for display.

3 Inventory the visual aids you use in teaching: pictures, objects, videos, on-site inspections, charts, maps, overhead transparencies, movies, TV programs, magazines, books. Keep a record of when you used each aid so as to insure variety and future use.

4 Invite an authority to come to your class who teaches by visual demonstration rather than lecture. Observe the attention and retention level of your students during and after. Give your students a quiz to measure their retention through visual observation.

Advanced

5 Create a visual aids center in your classroom to promote students' creation and use of visual aids in their assignments and projects. When they are responsible for reports or presentations, require visual aids based on the equipment you make available.

6 Teach your students discernment through a study of the media's use of visual aids in communicating subliminal messages through various methods. Bring in samples and discuss the spiritual and emotional power of the visual media.

a Chance

s some
dlock

AFFIRMATION

"Teach Like Christ"

The teacher who models his or her teaching methods after those of Christ is a teacher who teaches with style. Christ taught with authority, and no more so than when He delivered a **lecture**. As He gave the truth, He illustrated that truth with **stories** from life. He was able to teach wherever He went, because He always had **visual aids** at hand. To promote self-learning and deep thinking, Christ used **questions and answers** to pull His "students" along in their discovery of truth. And when those questions raised difficult issues, He was more likely to promote a **discussion** than solve the dilemma outright. And **drama!** Christ loved it, because it pictured truth in an unforgettable way. Christ also assigned **projects** so the disciples could put the truth to work.

The person who teaches like Christ is a person who Teaches with Style! By the grace of God, you can be that person!

You shall teach them diligently to your children, and shall talk of them when you sit in your house, when you walk by the way, when you lie down, and when you rise up.

Deuteronomy 6:7

I commit to Teach with Style through following the methodology of Christ—the practice of dynamic methods which, when used, result in LifeChange in my students.

2·16·02

Signature/Date

DIAGNOSTIC
CHARTS

The last point in Session One on Universal Principles of Style says that "Style is a learned skill and can be significantly improved through understanding and practice." Now that you have understanding, it's time to practice—with Style!

Practice Makes Perfect!

The four charts to which you were introduced in Session Four (External Behaviors) are reproduced on the following pages for your use. Ask a friend or fellow teacher to help you by recording your gestures, voice, and body and eye movements on the charts. In order to measure your progress, have someone fill out a set of charts on your style periodically, perhaps four times a year. Then compare the charts for progress and to note persistent "trouble spots." Learning new skills is much more enjoyable when progress is recorded, viewed, and appreciated over a significant length of time!

Permission Granted!

Walk Thru the Bible grants the owner of this Course Workbook permission to reproduce these charts (pages A-2 through A-5) for diagnostic evaluations of his or her personal teaching style. Please do not reproduce otherwise.

NOTE: Variation, or voice movement within the scales, is the ideal use of the voice.

TO THE EVALUATOR: After a few moments of listening, shade in the horizontal panel on each of the three gauges indicating where the speaker's volume, pitch, and rate "stays" most of the time. Then place individual dots above and below the "normal" panel to indicate each time the speaker diverts above or below the norm, and to what degree.

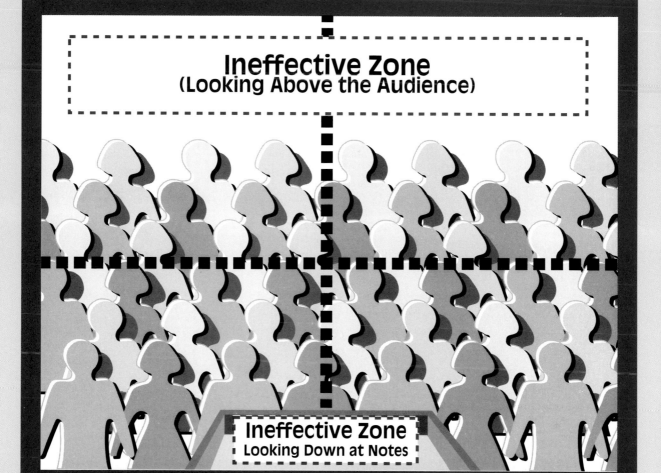

Ineffective Zone
(Looking Above the Audience)

Ineffective Zone
Looking Down at Notes

NOTE: Avoid the "Ineffective Zones" by talking to
the four quadrants of your audience.

TO THE EVALUATOR: From your vantage point in the audience, watch the speaker's eyes. Indicate with small check marks on this chart the faces where he or she focuses (be sure and indicate if the speaker's eyes stay in the Ineffective Zones). If the speaker uses the helpful technique of making and holding eye contact with an audience member for an extended time (15-20 seconds), draw a circle around a figure to represent that extended contact.

NOTE: Gestures should extend into all three spatial dimensions: height, width, and depth.

TO THE EVALUATOR: Indicate with a dot or small check each time a significant gesture is made, showing both the area and the degree of extension. Upon completion of the teaching session, use circles to group clusters of marks to show patterns and tendencies and to highlight "unused" areas. Clusters of marks close to the body indicate a need for practicing extension of the hands and arms.

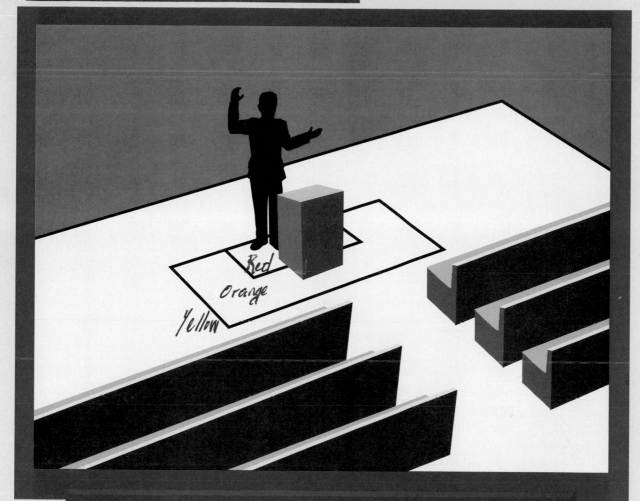

NOTE: Movement should be coupled with timing and mood for maximum effectiveness.

TO THE EVALUATOR: The Movement Chart tracks the speaker's extent of mobility and mood when teaching. Write words such as "normal," "excited," "serious," "humorous," "story," and other mood or activity indicators on the chart in the location where the speaker was when conveying that information or mood. Use check marks next to the words to indicate multiple instances of the same movement and mood combinations. Assess afterwards for the best combinations: behind the podium for lecture, near the audience for humor, rapid movement for exciting content, etc.

There Is One Law of Gravity. There Are Fourteen Laws of Teaching. These Fifteen Laws Will Keep Students in Their Seats. Guaranteed.

Two of America's most widely respected trainers of teachers, Dr. Howard Hendricks and Dr. Bruce Wilkinson, bring you a double-barreled dose of lifechange. These two courses, part of the *Applied Principles of Learning* curriculum, are sold complete with video tapes, textbook, Course Workbook, and Leader's Guide. *The 7 Laws of the Teacher* consists of seven video sessions, while *The 7 Laws of the Learner* contains fourteen video sessions. They have become the most-used teacher training seminar materials available. **To receive information on ordering these products, request a WTB catalog at the bottom of page A-8.**

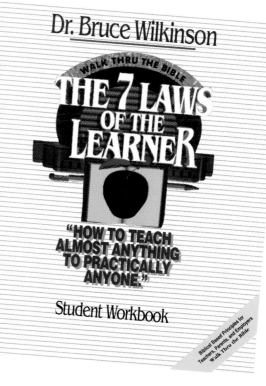

The APL Certificate of Achievement Recognizes Your Commitment. Go Ahead—You've Earned It!

Congratulations on taking an important step in your teaching ministry! By participating in the Teaching With Style seminar, you have made a commitment to lifechange— yours as well as the lives of those you teach.

To recognize your commitment and achievement, Walk Thru the Bible has prepared a beautiful APL Certificate of Achievement award suitable for framing. And it's FREE!

Complete both sides of this form and mail to: APL Certificate
Walk Thru the Bible
P.O. Box 627
Mt. Morris, IL 61054-8358

Please allow 6-8 weeks for delivery

Again, congratulations for completing this exciting step in learning to teach with style. The next chapter in your adventure in teaching is just beginning!

APL
APPLIED PRINCIPLES OF LEARNING

CERTIFICATE
OF
ACHIEVEMENT

This certificate is given to

for successfully completing the Walk Thru the Bible Ministries® course devoted to building excellence in teaching and communication skills:
The 7 Laws of the Learner.

Seminar Instructor

Date of Completion

Bruce H. Wilkinson
Bruce H. Wilkinson
President
Walk Thru the Bible Ministries

Seminar Sponsor

Order Form

Name _____	Your Age: ❑ 18 or below
	❑ 19-25
Address _____	❑ 26-40
	❑ 41-55
City/State/Zip _____	❑ 56 or above

Phone Home (   ) _____   Office (   ) _____

Occupation _____   Name of Church _____

E-mail Address_____   Avg. Sunday A.M. Attendance _____

We value your opinion. Please complete the questionnaire below before returning your Certificate Order Form to your seminar leader. (Photocopies prohibited)

1. What group(s) have you taught? (check all that apply)

- ☐ Sunday A.M. church
- ☐ Sunday P.M. church
- ☐ Wednesday P.M. church
- ☐ Sunday school class
- ☐ School classes
- ☐ College classes
- ☐ Graduate classes
- ☐ Other (please specify): _____
- ☐ Church Bible study group
- ☐ Home/neighborhood Bible study group
- ☐ Family

2. What age group(s) are you currently teaching? (check all that apply)

- ☐ Preschool or kindergarten
- ☐ Grades 1-6
- ☐ Grades 7-12
- ☐ College
- ☐ Young Adult
- ☐ Middle Adult
- ☐ Senior Adult
- ☐ Mixed Ages

3. How did you learn about the Teaching With Style Seminar?

- ☐ Received mailing at home
- ☐ Received brochure at church
- ☐ Received brochure from a ministry (e.g. Campus Crusade, Navigators)
- ☐ Heard radio announcement
- ☐ Saw newspaper announcement
- ☐ Saw brochure/poster at Christian bookstore
- ☐ Pastor/church leader invited me
- ☐ Other: _____

4. Where was the Teaching With Style Seminar held that you attended?

Location _____   Date _____

Teacher _____   Seminar Leader _____

5. How would you rate the Teaching With Style Seminar on a scale of 1-10?
(Circle your response: 10=excellent; 1=poor)

a. The Video Sessions with Dr. Bruce Wilkinson	1	2	3	4	5	6	7	8	9	10
b. *OR* Your WTB Seminar Instructor	1	2	3	4	5	6	7	8	9	10
b. The Interaction Questions	1	2	3	4	5	6	7	8	9	10
c. The Daily Devotionals	1	2	3	4	5	6	7	8	9	10
d. The Application Projects	1	2	3	4	5	6	7	8	9	10
e. Your Video Seminar Leader	1	2	3	4	5	6	7	8	9	10

6. Please add your comments: _____
_____

Would you like to know more about Walk Thru the Bible products?

☐ Yes, please send me Walk Thru the Bible's catalog. I'd like to know more about WTB's devotional magazines, Bibles, Bible study aids, Old and New Testament Seminars, other APL seminars, and other video products.

OR CALL (800) 763-5433